COMBINED LEADER'S GUIDE

for *Before* "I DO" *and*
CATHOLIC *Remarriage*

Combined Leader's Guide

for Before "I Do" and CATHOLIC Remarriage

Anthony Garascia

ave maria press notre dame, indiana

Nihil obstat: Rev. Augustine DiNoia, O.P.; Mr. Fred Everett, Mrs. Lisa Everett; Rev. Jerome Listecki; Rev. Val Peter; Daniel Scheidt; Prof. Janet Smith; Rev. Peter Uglietto.

Imprimatur: Most Rev. John M. D'Arcy
              Bishop of Fort Wayne-South Bend
              November 1, 1998, Feast of All Saints

The *Imprimatur* is an official declaration that a book or pamphlet is free of doctrinal or moral error. No implication is contained therein that those who have granted the *Imprimatur* agree with its contents, opinions, or statements expressed.

Excerpts from *This Is Our Faith* by Michael Pennock © 1998 Ave Maria Press, used by permission. Excerpts from *The Church, Our Story* by Patricia Morrison Driedger © 1999, 2006 Ave Maria Press, used by permission.

Scripture texts used in this work are taken from *The New American Bible* copyright © 1991, 1986, and 1970 by the Confraternity of Christian Doctrine, Washington, DC, and are used by permission of the copyright owner. All rights reserved. No part of *The New American Bible* may be reproduced in any form or by any means without permission in writing from the publisher.

Founded in 1865, Ave Maria Press is a ministry of the Indiana Province of Holy Cross. www.avemariapress.com

ISBN-10 1-59471-142-9 ISBN-13 978-1-59471-142-8

Cover and text design by David R. Scholtes

Printed and bound in the United States of America.

I wish to express my appreciation to Eileen Ponder for her helpful suggestions and support in producing this new addition and to Bob Hamma who has been helpful in producing all of my marriage preparation materials with Ave Maria Press.

Contents

Foreword:
What Three Thousand Couples Taught Me About Marriage

Having been involved with marriage preparation on a diocesan level for over thirty years, I've listened to the hopes and expectations, concerns and disappointments of over three thousand engaged couples. It is an honor to be trusted as an advisor at such an important step in a couple's life. It can also be a burden. As marriage has become more complex and lost some societal support, it's painful to see the breakup of marriages that started out full of hope and promise. It is especially tragic to witness the relationships that could have been saved or painful arguments that could have been handled more constructively had the engaged couple only had better preparation or a trusted mentor to turn to during troubled times. What I've learned from helping prepare over three thousand couples for marriage is that they could surely use programs like *Before "I Do"* and *Catholic Remarriage*.

Currently, I teach a course called "Christian Marriage" to university students. It is encouraging to hear their optimism as they consider how they will resolve conflicts in their own marriages. Unfortunately, it's often also unrealistic. A common response I hear is, "We'll just work it out because we will love and respect each other. We'll compromise." If only love and marriage were that simple. In *Before "I Do"* and *Catholic Remarriage*, Anthony Garascia helps couples challenge the myths of "happily ever after." He doesn't do it in a preachy, moralistic way, however. He does it by asking the right questions. Case studies and well-crafted questions guide the couple to explore their own growing relationship. As couples get to peek into real marriages through the case studies, they can then ask themselves how they would respond if faced with a lessening of romance, an alcoholic spouse, or a conflict over who's pulling their weight in the marriage.

Not only do *Before "I Do"* and *Catholic Remarriage* help engaged or newly-wed couples examine the thorny issues of marriage but they also blend the secular with the sacred. Sacramental marriage is not only thinking through what one would do in conflict situations. It must also include the best of human psychology and awaken or deepen a faith commitment. Garascia introduces couples to the influences that their families of origin, family systems, and each partner's unique personality will have on their marriage. These are sociological and counseling insights that have only recently been applied to marital relationship theory.

As St. Thomas Aquinas said, "Grace builds on nature." So the more couples know about the natural dynamics of human interactions, the better they can enter into a mature marriage relationship. Add to this the wisdom and inspiration of our Catholic heritage, and we pray that the grace will flow into each of the couples who work with *Before "I Do"* or *Catholic Remarriage.* Yes, the total self-giving and unconditional, faithful, lifelong love of marriage is a pretty impossible promise when looked at on solely a human level, but "nothing is impossible with God." Before "I do" and even *after* "I do," couples will find these books grace-filled companions on their journeys together.

Susan Vogt

Author, Speaker, Relationship Coach

1

Getting Started

THE GOALS OF THESE PROGRAMS

Welcome to the *Combined Leader's Guide for Before "I Do" and Catholic Remarriage*, two programs designed to assist priests, deacons, and a variety of lay pastoral ministers who collaborate in various ways in the proximate preparation of engaged couples for marriage. *Before "I Do"* (for those entering marriage for the first time) and *Catholic Remarriage* (for those preparing for remarriage or convalidation following annulment) are, first and foremost, pastoral programs. As such, they do not aim to provide a fully developed theology of marriage, or to make up for whatever may be missing in a couple's catechetical formation and understanding of the faith. They do, however, aim to be resources assisting those working in marriage preparation ministries whom the Rite of Marriage calls to "strengthen and nourish the faith of those who are about to be married, for the sacrament of marriage presupposes and demands faith."[1]

The introduction to the rite further specifies that the priest who will witness a marriage should first offer the couple "a review of the fundamentals of Christian doctrine. This may include instruction on the teaching about marriage and the family, on the rites used in the celebration of the sacrament itself, and on the prayers and readings."[2] While the aim of these programs is to assist in this process, they do not claim to be comprehensive treatments of these issues. Because there is a wide range of understanding with regard to the fundamentals of Christian doctrine, the priest or deacon presiding at the wedding needs to assess the couple's need in this area. This leader's guide also presumes that the priest or deacon witnessing the marriage will engage the couple with planning the wedding liturgy itself. Numerous resources are available for liturgy planning, including *Together for Life* (also available from Ave Maria Press).

The Committee on Marriage and Family Life at the United States Conference of Catholic Bishops began the National Pastoral Initiative on Marriage in 2005. The Initiative seeks to bring Catholic tradition about the meaning and value of married life into dialogue with contemporary needs. As the Initiative was being considered, Bishop J. Kevin Boland, chair of the Committee on Marriage and Family Life, cited these recent statistics on marriage in the United States.

- More than 80% of adults say that having a good marriage is absolutely necessary for them to consider their life a success (Family Research Council).

- There was a 48% drop in Church-recorded marriages between 1984 and 2004, according to the 2004 Official Catholic Directory.

- During that same period, the annual rate of all marriages in the U. S. declined by 24% (National Center for Health Statistics).

- The median age of a first marriage is twenty-five for women and twenty-seven for men (National Marriage Project).

- For couples marrying today, the lifetime probability of divorce remains close to 50% (National Marriage Project).

- Being well educated, having a decent income, coming from an intact family, being religiously observant, and marrying after age twenty-five without having a baby first are all factors that lower one's chances of divorce to less than 50% (National Marriage Project).

- On average, people who end their first marriage do so in their early thirties (Barna Group Research Report).

- Among all adults who have been married, 35% have also been divorced. Of those who have divorced, 18% have done so more than once (Barna Group Research Report).

- Among the baby-boom generation, born between 1946 and 1960, 46% have already lived through divorce at least once (Barna Group Research Report).

- The number of annulment cases brought to diocesan and regional tribunals worldwide in 2002 was 54,247. Of this number, the total in the United States was 30,845 (Vatican Statistical Yearbook of the Catholic Church).

- Catholics are still less likely to get divorced than Protestants, by 25% to 39% (Barna Group Research Report).

- Over 80% of those seeking to be married in the Catholic Church in the United States (over 200,000 annually) participate in a marriage preparation program (USCCB surveys).

Obviously, as a priest, deacon, or lay pastoral minister charged with helping couples prepare for marriage, you face an immense task. In his 1981 apostolic exhortation *On the Family*, Pope John Paul II called the Church to provide greater pastoral care for those preparing for marriage:

> The Church must therefore promote better and more extensive programs of marriage preparation in order to eliminate as far as possible the difficulties that many married couples find themselves in, and even more to favor positively the establishing and maturing of successful marriages.[3]

The primary aim of *Before "I Do"* and *Catholic Remarriage* is to help engaged couples prepare for the commitment and responsibilities that the sacrament of marriage entails. This *Combined Leader's Guide* will help you, as a marriage preparation minister, learn how to make the best use of the materials contained in the couples' workbooks.

BEFORE "I DO"

The approach of this program is primarily pastoral. *Before "I Do"* attempts to tap into the excitement and enthusiasm already present in the engaged couple and to focus that energy into building a spiritual foundation for marriage, a foundation that will last. It seeks to constantly remind couples that marriage is more than the wedding—that it is a lived reality embedded in the mystery of the triune God who calls us to the fullness of life in Christ through the Holy Spirit.

Three aspects comprise this pastoral approach to marriage preparation. These three areas are built upon the latest research into the most effective marriage preparation programs. They are:

1. Facilitation of Insight and Awareness

The program attempts to facilitate a process whereby the engaged couple gains insight into the influences that have shaped the two of them through the years, and how these influences affect the way they interact with each other in the present. Many engaged couples already come into marriage preparation with a good amount of energy and insight. In this case the task is to validate and affirm the energy and awareness already present in the engaged couples. However, as the saying goes, "love is blind." Engaged couples don't always see everything about how they interact and are often grateful when they learn something important about themselves in the course of their preparation.

2. Relational Skills

Insight into oneself is often sufficient to initiate change and to foster a deeper commitment to the process of building a mature relationship. However, actual skill building is also an essential component, especially in the areas of communication and conflict resolution. Many engaged and married couples have underdeveloped skills in this area or have learned unhealthy and harmful ways of communication from their families of origin. These unhealthy patterns can block the development of a mature relationship, and in the extreme lead to the downfall of the marriage.

3. Placing Spirituality as a Significant Component to Marriage Preparation

This program is built around the belief that an understanding of and a commitment to grow in a Catholic Christian spirituality are essential for a lasting marriage. As a result, each of the six sessions in this program includes a section on the spirituality of marriage. Further, sessions 2 through 6 begin with a reflection on some dimension of the sacramentality of marriage. A wholehearted, positive embrace of the spirituality of Catholic marriage can be a positive and efficacious reality for the engaged couple. Too often we downplay the wisdom of our tradition because one of the engaged parties is a member of another Christian denomination, or because we are a little embarrassed to talk about our faith. As this discomfort fades, an engaged couple will begin to expect to talk about spirituality and will even miss this aspect if it is not included.

THE DESIGN OF THE PROGRAM

This program is written for two different types of implementation, the couple-to-couple approach and the group preparation approach. While both approaches have the same goals, their methodologies vary enough so as to call for separate implementation notes. Both approaches are given fuller treatment below.

1. The Couple-to-Couple Approach

In this model, the engaged couple is assigned to a married couple in the parish or other pastoral setting (e.g., campus ministry). The married couple is often referred to as the **lead couple**, as this couple will take leadership in facilitating the interaction between the engaged couple and themselves. Once assigned, the lead couple makes contact with the engaged couple and sets up the first appointment or sessions.

Sessions are usually held in the lead couple's home, although they may sometimes be scheduled at a more neutral site like a parish office. The benefit of meeting in the lead couple's home is that the engaged couple gets to see firsthand the workings of an established household with all of its uniqueness. It can be important, for instance, for an engaged couple to witness firsthand how the lead couple handles things like bedtime for their own children.

Most couple-to-couple programs are four to six sessions in length, with individual sessions taking from ninety minutes to two hours. The benefits to this type of an approach are obvious: the engaged couple gets a one-on-one opportunity to reflect on how they have prepared for marriage thus far and an opportunity to continue the preparation over the next four to six sessions. The engaged couple also has the opportunity of learning from the experiences of the married couple. It often happens that many engaged couples develop close ties with their lead couple, and it is not unusual for them to stay in touch months and sometimes years after their wedding date.

The disadvantages of a couple-to-couple approach are few. The most serious drawback to this type of program occurs when either the right "chemistry" does not occur between the engaged and lead couples or when one member (or both) of the engaged couple comes into the program resistant or resentful at having to participate. These issues will be addressed in chapter 4 of this manual.

2. The Group Approach

This approach calls for several or even many engaged couples to come and participate in a program designed to provide both private and group reflection on the topic of marriage. In this approach, a **marriage preparation team** usually takes responsibility for the planning and implementation of the day. Some members of the team may have specific responsibilities such as giving talks, while others may serve as facilitators of the small group reflection.

The length of the program varies with each one's objectives. Some programs cover eight to ten hours in a day or weekend, while others cover much more time over a series of gatherings. The second approach allows for more group process where engaged couples tell stories and get to meet other couples with similar interests and goals.

Some group programs include a presentation on a given topic by a guest speaker, or speakers. Thus, if the topic for the evening were conflict, it would be expected that someone—usually a married couple—would make a presentation on the topic. The presentation would cover two aspects: personal sharing on how the couple dealt with the topic in their own lives and practical information concerning the topic. In the case of the topic of conflict, the participants would receive some useful hints about how to handle conflict in their own relationship.

One of the benefits of a group program is the rapport that can develop between the engaged couples who participate in the program. In this setting, team members can intentionally plan opportunities for mixing and sharing between the couples with the expectation that interpersonal learning will occur. The fact that everyone is united around the common task of preparing for marriage also creates a sense of camaraderie that can be utilized by the team.

This approach can have shortcomings, especially if the group of participants is too large and the leadership team does not have the necessary leadership skills. Then the group process will hinder, not facilitate, rapport between couples. Teams need especially to try to be aware of designing group processes that match the maturity and age level of the participants. While avoiding "gimmicks," group processes should invite participants into an ever-deepening sharing of their experience.

The Use of Pre-marriage Inventories in a Marriage Prep Program

Research has shown that the most helpful marriage preparation involves a combination of "clergy, parish staff, and lay couples."[4] In this ideal form of marriage preparation each party involved assumes a distinct role. Often a priest or deacon will meet with a couple to begin the proximate preparation, which includes establishing general expectations for marriage preparation as well as specific expectations for the wedding itself. Either the clergy person himself or a staff person will usually administer a premarital inventory and schedule subsequent meetings to interpret the survey for the couple. As this process gets underway, the couple is then referred to either a parish program or a weekend experience such as Engaged Encounter.

Marriage preparation inventories are instruments that cover a comprehensive set of themes dealing with the skills required for a successful marriage. The themes include communication, extended family, interreligious marriages, conflict resolution, personality, and key problem areas such as substance abuse and physical abuse. Participants who take the inventories are most often asked to agree or disagree with various statements on a particular theme. For instance, one statement might read: "I am concerned about the amount of alcohol that my partner consumes." If both check "disagree" then that item would not be flagged for discussion, since this would not emerge as a problem area. If either partner checks "agree," that question would be flagged, and the pastoral minister who administered the inventory would most probably pursue this as an issue for discussion.

Premarital inventories are a good tool for identifying areas for special discussion. They also give the couple feedback about how alike or unlike each person is to the other on a wide range of issues. When there is a high degree of similarity in both partners' responses to the inventory, the couple is often affirmed in their readiness for marriage. A high degree of dissimilarity in responses can become an opportunity to raise specific issues of readiness. In this case the pastoral minister will sometimes refer the couple for counseling so that they can work out whatever unresolved issues are raised.

The premarital inventory can be seen as the first step in proximate marriage preparation. It should normally precede the second step of attending either the parish's marriage prep program or one sponsored or approved by the diocese. In this second stage there is not as much opportunity to pursue specific questions and issues in depth. The use of an inventory and the experience of working with someone trained to interpret it provide an opportunity to alert the couple to potential trouble areas that remain hidden from their view. The marriage prep program, on the other hand, allows for interpersonal sharing of stories and learning from other married couples the "way of marriage." Here, the task of the lead couple or team members is not to ferret out unresolved issues as much as to invite the engaged couple to enter into a stance of reflective sharing and listening that deepens the bond between them and gives them a different perspective on issues that may be important to sustaining their commitment.

2

The Various Ministries Involved in Marriage Preparation

In his encyclical entitled *On the Family* (*Familiaris Consortio*), Pope John Paul II stated: "The person principally responsible in the diocese for the pastoral care of the family is the bishop."[5] He goes on to outline how the Church provides pastoral care for families as well as its role in the preparation of engaged couples for marriage. He outlines three distinct periods of preparation for marriage: remote preparation, involving the experience of living in a family that provides a living testimony to what a marriage is; proximate preparation, involving the ongoing religious education and formation of the person through the years leading to adulthood; and immediate preparation, involving the parish priest, marriage preparation program, music director (if available), parish wedding coordinator (if available), and other laypeople who may assist the parish in its celebration of the sacrament of marriage.

Each diocese implements the Vatican's directives in different and distinct ways according to the particular needs of its people. Most often, since the bishop cannot personally become involved in the specific immediate preparation of every engaged couple, he has delegated this responsibility to his priests, who in turn enlist the help of the laity to assist in the preparation of an engaged couple.

THE ROLE OF THE PRIEST OR DEACON

The United States Conference of Catholic Bishops has identified two principal areas of concern for the clergy person who is preparing a couple for marriage: that of discerning the presence of faith on the part of the couple approaching him for the sacrament and that of determining that the couple is ready and free to marry.[6] The priest's or deacon's role is an essential one.

He represents the bishop and has the responsibility to ensure that a couple approaching the sacrament meets the criteria outlined by the Church for a valid reception of the sacrament.

In dioceses with a shortage of priests, the bishop may delegate these responsibilities to a permanent deacon. If this occurs, the deacon is the person given official jurisdiction over how marriage preparation is to be implemented at the local parish. Other dioceses face the shortage of both priests and permanent deacons and may turn to a religious brother, sister, or other lay ecclesial minister (LEM) to serve in an "extraordinary" capacity as the pastoral administrator or parish life coordinator. In this case the religious brother, sister, or other lay ecclesial minister is delegated by the bishop and serves at his request. This is why, throughout this manual, the phrase, "priest, deacon, or designated LEM" is used.

The Criteria of Faith

The issue of discerning whether faith is present seems, at first glance, a simple thing. Either you have faith or you don't. Yet the pope and National Conference of Catholic Bishops recognize that faith exists on many different levels and may be manifested in a "seminal" or preconscious way.[7] Even a couple that appears to be marrying in the Church for only "social" reasons (a church wedding "looks good" to family) may indeed have the seeds of faith deeply implanted.

The role of the priest, deacon, or designated LEM in this regard is not so much to challenge and refuse but to invite and be hospitable to the couple and encourage their continued growth in faith and spirituality. In the end, the Church tends toward leniency in assessing the faith life of the engaged couple. The only time when a priest, deacon, or pastoral minister has a duty to refuse the sacrament of marriage is when "an engaged couple explicitly and formally reject what the Church intends to do in the marriage of baptized persons."[8] Fr. Joseph Champlin sums up the Church's attitude very well:

> Priests, deacons, and pastoral ministers need to challenge, but not crush those who come to them seeking the sacraments and services of the Church. They need to be at one and the same time, both teachers and shepherds, simultaneously holding up the ideal,

while reaching out to marginal Catholics. They need to be prophets, proclaiming God's message with consistency, truth, and courage, yet searching for stray members with compassion, mercy, and forgiveness. In preaching the demands of justice and holiness, they need, above all, to be like their Master, the suffering servant Messiah, extremely careful not break the bruised reed or to snuff out the smoldering wick.[9]

Readiness and Freedom to Marry

The second clearly defined role of the priest, deacon, or designated LEM is to assess the couple's readiness and freedom to marry. This is a serious obligation because the entire theology of the sacrament depends on the couple making an intentional decision to enter into a marriage in the way that the Church understands marriage. In order to enter into marriage a person must have the necessary emotional maturity and be free of any serious impediment that might compromise his or her freedom to bring about the marriage bond.

In the initial meetings with the couple the priest, deacon, or pastoral minister must be convinced that both parties are indeed free to marry: that there has been no previous bond of marriage, that the individuals are of sound mind (no serious psychological illnesses that might impede freedom), that they are not under undue pressure to marry (in the case of a pregnancy, for instance), and that they both possesses sufficient maturity to intentionally enter into the bond of marriage. This duty is taken seriously, even to the extent of an official "prenuptial investigation" whose only purpose is to determine a couple's freedom to marry.

The issue of psychological readiness or maturity is more difficult to assess than, for instance, an obvious impediment such as a previous marriage. The priest, deacon, or designated LEM has available to him or her resources such as premarital inventories that will identify serious issues that might impede a person's ability to give free and irrevocable consent to the marriage. In the event that a person is judged not psychologically ready for marriage, the National Conference of Catholic Bishops' guidelines make it clear that the sacrament of marriage can only be refused for as long as the cause for refusal exists.

> The Revised Code of Canon Law decrees that all persons not prohibited by law can contract marriage. It does, nevertheless, empower the local ordinary to prohibit a person's marriage, but only for a time and for a serious cause—for as long as the cause exists. Dioceses with a common policy of selective postponement for the ill-prepared cite this empowerment as the legal basis for such a procedure.[10]

For instance, in the case of a person who experiences a serious depressive illness, a priest might recommend postponement of the marriage until the affected party has received sufficient treatment. Once treatment has demonstrated that this is no longer an impediment to a free consent, then the marriage can take place.

The Purposes of Marriage

There is one further role that the priest, deacon, or designated LEM assumes. This minister is to ensure that the couple is entering into a marriage that conforms to the Church's teaching regarding the twofold meaning of marriage: mutual and lasting fidelity between the spouses and the procreation of children. The prenuptial investigation includes questions that cover a person's intention to enter a permanent marriage that can be dissolved only by death and an understanding that one purpose of marriage is the begetting and rearing of children.[11] Here, if a couple answers "no" to either of these questions, the priest, deacon, or pastoral minister is bound to refuse the sacrament because no marriage, in fact, can take place.

It also falls to the priest, deacon, or pastoral minister to raise with the engaged couple the issue of family planning. The U.S. Conference of Catholic Bishops has stressed that marriage preparation should include teaching and information on responsible family planning, including guidance to the couple on what it means to form a mature conscience. Its criteria for a mature conscience involves attitudes of generosity, trust, humility, and mutuality, and decisions based on the wisdom and guidance of the Church.[12] It also emphasizes that natural methods of family planning are the only methods approved by the Church. Many dioceses encourage engaged couples to attend a Natural Family Planning workshop before their marriage so that they can learn more about the advantages of choosing this method of family planning.

As expressed in the encyclical letter *On Human Life* (*Humane Vitae*) in 1968, the Church's teaching on the issue of artificial contraception is clear. Unfortunately, many couples view the Church's teaching on this issue as a judgment on them rather than as an invitation. The Church's teaching on this issue has a very real pastoral dimension, offering assistance and guidance to couples, many of whom are not fully aware of the values upheld by the Church's teaching on this subject.

It must be emphasized, when all is said and done, that the Church holds that a baptized person has a right to the sacrament of marriage. Poorly developed faith, getting married for "cultural reasons," and other mixed motives are not in themselves reasons to deny a person the sacrament. As the bishops have stated: "The faith of the person seeking marriage in the Church can exist in varying degrees. It is the primary duty of pastors to facilitate a rediscovery of this faith, nourishing it and bringing it to maturity."[13]

THE ROLE OF THE MARRIAGE PREPARATION PROGRAM

A marriage preparation program is an important help to an engaged couple's immediate preparation for marriage, but in itself it is not essential to an engaged couple's readiness for marriage. A priest, deacon, or designated LEM doesn't send an engaged couple to a marriage prep program in order to assess their readiness to marry. Rather, he or she first assesses their readiness, and then sends them on to a marriage prep program only if he or she believes them ready to marry. We must be careful not to assign too high of an expectation and/or importance to marriage preparation programs. They can assist a couple to be better prepared, but most of the work of getting ready to marry has already been done by the couple in the months or years preceding their decision to marry. Perhaps even more significantly, individuals prepare for marriage in a remote way by growing up in a family with parents whose own marriage forms much of what one believes and values about marriage.

On the one hand, marriage preparation programs are an important tool in assisting the couple to deepen their love, faith, and preparation for marriage. On the other hand, we can't legitimately expect them to fully catechize a couple in the theology of marriage or be an evaluative tool whereby we try to "test" the readiness of a couple. These programs simply assist the Church in helping a couple be better prepared.

The National Conference of Catholic Bishops reflected on the balance between a couple's readiness, faith development, and the role of marriage preparation programs:

> Pope John Paul II places this delicate issue of the engaged couple's faith and readiness in perspective when he both urges better and more intense programs of marriage preparation and stresses their necessity and obligation, yet cautions that omitting them is not an impediment to the celebration of marriage.[14]

Then why have a marriage prep program in the first place? Because research has shown that 50 percent of marriages that fail do so within the first seven years of marriage, it makes sense to do whatever we can to bolster the readiness of a couple so that they can weather the inevitable strains that will test their relationship. Also, the fact that the local Church expends so much time and energy in helping a couple prepare for marriage paves the way for a positive future relationship not only with the parish where the marriage is celebrated but with any parish where the couple may live in the future. Given a good experience in marriage prep, a young married couple might be more inclined to turn to the Church should their marriage experience turbulence in the early years.

Research has indicated that the best form of marriage preparation is that of a team format. A study done by the Center for Marriage and Family at Creighton University stated:

> Marriage preparation is perceived as most valuable when a team administers it. Clergy working alone with a couple continues to be the most common format for administering marriage preparation, and it is perceived as a valuable format. In this study, however, respondents perceived it as a significantly less valuable format than administration by a team. A team make-up of clergy, lay couples, and parish staff was the instructor combination that yielded the highest perceived values. To be noted here is the critical role of clergy on this team. Respondents judged the absence of clergy from the marriage preparation process to be seriously detrimental to the process.[15]

It would appear, therefore, that a combination of clergy and lay involvement in the marriage preparation process is one of the most important things a parish can provide for its engaged couples. The priest or deacon usually presents the Church's teachings on marriage and gives official sanction to the decision of an engaged couple to seek marriage in the first place. The laity on the team serve as witnesses to the qualities of faith, fidelity, and the other virtues that go into forming a successful and long-standing marriage. They also bear witness to the practical, day-to-day issues in developing a spirituality of marriage.

This marriage preparation program seeks to foster the ideal outlined above whereby a team of clergy and laity work together to ensure the best possible preparation of an engaged couple. In this model there are clearly defined roles: the priest, deacon, or designated LEM assumes responsibility for giving ecclesial affirmation of the couple and for sharing with them the essentials of the Church's teaching on marriage. The lead couple or team members assist in the formation by their witness and by taking the engaged couple through a program aimed at skill building and insight awareness. The engaged couple's book is meant to address only this latter role in the marriage preparation process. It does not seek to present a complete catechesis on the sacrament of marriage and presumes that the priest, deacon, or designated LEM will present such a teaching in accordance with his or her assessment of the couple's needs.

The couple's book is more oriented to practical skill building and awareness while encouraging the participants to take seriously the deepening of their spirituality. It is not meant to be a course on either the theology or spirituality of marriage, although from time to time certain theological and spiritual issues may be raised for consideration by the couple.

THE ROLE OF THE LITURGIST, MUSIC DIRECTOR, AND/OR WEDDING COORDINATOR

Many parishes today employ a liturgist or music director who is responsible for organizing the wedding music. This person will probably meet with the engaged couple to begin the initial planning of the wedding liturgy and to select the music. Parishes are subject to diocesan guidelines on music for weddings, should any exist. Thus, one role of the music director may be to exercise a veto over music that the couple might want but that is not suitable for liturgical celebration. Often, there will be a brochure or small booklet made available to the engaged couple as soon as they schedule their wedding so that problems can be anticipated early and planned for. Some engaged couples don't understand the reasons why some of their songs are rejected, and it behooves the parish staff and especially the liturgist or music director to have a well-thought-out policy that can be easily explained.

In some parishes there is a wedding coordinator who serves as the overall coordinator of parish ministries to the engaged. In large parishes this relieves the priest, deacon, or designated LEM of a lot of important but nonessential work. For instance, if there is a worship booklet to be typed up, the wedding coordinator might oversee that. Also, in large parishes that might have two to three weddings a week, a wedding coordinator can ensure that each party understands basic things like where to dress, when to arrive, how much time it has for pictures after the wedding, and when it needs to leave the church so that the next wedding party can begin its immediate preparations for the liturgy.

OTHER PROFESSIONALS

Another valuable service to parishes today is that of the professional counselor who is experienced in relationship counseling and who may have a particular specialty in working with engaged couples. Often, the local Catholic Charities office works closely with parishes to provide services of this type. Also, there are usually local therapists and/or counselors who specialize in this field and who are sympathetic to the goals and values of the Church in preparing couples for marriage. These professionals can be very helpful to the marriage preparation team, especially when there is concern about readiness for marriage.

3

Understanding the Sacrament of Marriage

While the role of the lead couple or team in a marriage preparation program is not to provide religious education for the engaged, married couples often find that as the level of trust and comfort grows, the engaged couple will raise questions about the Church's teaching on marriage. The aim of this section is to offer lead couples and teams some background so that they may be better able to present the Church's vision of marriage in their sharing with the engaged. There may be times when it will be helpful to suggest that the engaged couple discuss their questions and concerns with the priest or deacon presiding at their wedding, yet there will be other occasions when married couples, because of their lived experience, can indeed be the best teachers of the faith.

The material in the first section of this chapter is excerpted from a widely used catechism *This Is Our Faith* by Michael Pennock.[16] The book follows closely the *Catechism of the Catholic Church* (CCC). The second section of this chapter, "A Sacred Covenant, a Holy Sacrament," is the author's own theological reflection on marriage in light of Vatican II and the revised Rite of Marriage issued after the Council. Finally, a brief history of how marriage has been celebrated in the Catholic Church is offered. This material is based on *The Church: Our Story* by Patricia Morrison Driedger.[17]

MARRIAGE: WHAT THE CHURCH TEACHES AND BELIEVES

What Is the Sacrament of Matrimony? (CCC, 1601; 1660)

In the sacrament of matrimony a baptized man and woman vow their love in an exclusive, permanent, sexual partnership. This union is marked by love, respect, care and concern, and a commitment to share responsibility in the raising of a family if God should bless them with children.

The matrimonial covenant, by which a man and a woman establish between themselves a partnership of the whole of life, is by its nature ordered toward the good of the spouses and the procreation and the education of offspring; this covenant between baptized persons has been raised by Christ the Lord to the dignity of a sacrament. For this reason, a matrimonial contract cannot validly exist between baptized persons unless it is also a sacrament by that fact. (Canon 1055)

Christian marriage is an extraordinary sign of God working through and in the ordinary. Christ Jesus has raised marriage to the dignity of a sacrament. Simply put, a good marriage is not only like a civil contract between two persons but is also a holy covenant involving three persons. Jesus Christ, who promises to bless, sustain, and rejoice in their union, joins the couple on their life's journey.

What Does the Old Testament Say About Marriage? (CCC, 1602–1608)

The vocation of marriage is written in the very nature of men and women, who are created by a God of infinite love. Original sin, however, taints God's intent for the harmonious loving between men and women. Thus, men and women must seek God's grace to achieve the loving unity God intends for them.

Through the period of the original Covenant, there was a gradual growth in understanding of the meaning of marriage. In early times polygamy was tolerated; husbands could freely divorce their wives (who were often treated as property). By the time the book of Genesis was written, however, God revealed to the Jewish people two profound truths about the purposes of marriage. First, marriage is a share in God's creative purpose of bringing new life into the world.

God created man in his image;
in the divine image he created him;
male and female he created them.
God blessed them, saying: "Be fertile and multiply;
fill the earth and subdue it. Have dominion over the
    fish of the sea,

the birds of the air, and all the living things that move
  on the earth."
God looked at everything he had made, and he found
  it very good.
Evening came, and morning followed—the sixth day.

—Genesis 1:27–28, 31

Second, marriage creates a new relationship—one that was not there be-fore—between a husband and wife. Genesis also reveals this other major purpose of marriage—companionship between friends who share the same life and love:

The man said: "This one, at last, is bone of my bones
and flesh of my flesh;
This one shall be called 'woman,' for out of 'her man'
this one has been taken."
That is why a man leaves his father and mother
and clings to his wife,
and the two of them become one body.

—Genesis 2:23–24

God fully intends a permanent, exclusive, monogamous relationship be-tween man and woman, who have been created in the divine image.

How Does Marriage Mirror God's Love for Us? (CCC, 1609–1611)

Divine mercy would not allow God to forsake humans tainted by sin. Although pain in childbirth and the need to toil by "the sweat of your brow" were two effects of original sin, God uses marriage to help man and woman "to overcome self-absorption, egoism, pursuit of one's own pleasure, and to open oneself to the other, to mutual aid and to self-giving" (CCC, 1609).

The prophets use marriage as an image to describe Yahweh's great love for his people, Israel.

I will espouse you to me forever:
I will espouse you in right and in justice,
in love and in mercy;
I will espouse you in fidelity,
and you shall know the LORD.

—Hosea 2:21

The prophet Malachi forcefully states the ideal:

> Because the LORD is witness between you and the wife of your youth, with whom you have broken faith though she is your companion, your betrothed wife. Did he not make one being, with flesh and spirit: and what does that one require but godly offspring? You must then safeguard life that is your own, and not break faith with the wife of your youth.
>
> —Malachi 2:14–15

Proverbs paints a picture of an ideal wife: "She is clothed in strength and dignity" (Prv 31:25). The books of Ruth and Tobit highlight the fidelity and tenderness of spouses. The Song of Songs describes love between a bride and a bridegroom. Because God has blessed marriage, affectionate, erotic love between a husband and wife is something good and holy and joyful.

What Does the New Testament Reveal About Marriage? (CCC, 1613–1616; 1659)

The New Testament reveals further important insights into the nature of marriage. Jesus' attendance at the wedding feast of Cana underscores the goodness and naturalness of marriage. When Jesus teaches about marriage, he reaffirms the original intention of his Father—that marriage should be a permanent, exclusive love relationship: "Everyone who divorces his wife and marries another commits adultery, and the one who marries a woman divorced from her husband commits adultery" (Lk 16:18).

Jesus shows his profound respect for human dignity when he teaches that looking at a woman lustfully is the equivalent of committing adultery (Mt 5:27–28). Motives and interior attitudes are important to him.

The early church also regarded marriage highly. St. Paul, for example, supplies a key teaching on marriage:

> So [also] husbands should love their wives as their own bodies. He who loves his wife loves himself. For no one hates his own flesh but rather nourishes and cherishes it, even as Christ does the church, because we are members of his body. "For this reason a man shall leave [his] father and [his] mother and be joined

to his wife, and the two shall become one flesh." This
is a great mystery, but I speak in reference to Christ
and the church.

—Ephesians 5:28–32

The union of a husband and wife is like the union of Christ with his church. St. Paul calls this reality a mystery (a word translated by St. Augustine as "sacrament"). Christian marriage is an external sign of Christ's love. Marriage is a covenant, a total lifelong commitment that mirrors Christ's love for his church.

How Is Marriage a Covenant? (CCC, 1612; 1617; 1661)

The Church teaches us that the sacrament of marriage mirrors God's covenant of love with his people. By giving us his Son, the Father loves us freely and faithfully keeps his promises to us. Jesus—the greatest sign of God's love—draws us into community, showers us with unexpected gifts, relates to us as unique individuals, and invites us to grow in love by serving others.

In the covenant of Christian marriage, a husband and wife freely bind themselves together for life. Theirs is an open-ended commitment to love exclusively. No time conditions or any other conditions are put on their relationship. In sickness or health, in poverty or wealth, in good times and in bad times, the couple promises to be faithful. A marriage covenant commitment mirrors God's unconditional love for his people. If a man and woman insist on certain conditions when getting married, they are simply engaged in a legal contract.

In Christian marriage love is freely given and faithfully weathers the trials that come its way. Christian marriage is life-giving because through it God gives the married couple the privilege of procreating.

It is full of surprises, providing countless opportunities to grow in holiness.

It is a concrete way to live the Christian life of love and service in the context of family living.

It is a place to receive the Lord, who showers the couple with the grace to love each other with the very love he has for the Church. This grace perfects the human love of the spouses, strengthens their indissoluble unity, and sanctifies them on their journey to eternal life.

How Is the Sacrament of Matrimony Celebrated? (CCC, 1621–1624; 1663)

In Christian marriage, the spouses are the ministers of the sacrament. They mutually confer the sacrament on one another by exchanging marriage vows before a witness of the Church. When both bride and groom are Catholic, marriage should usually take place during Mass (see the *Rite of Marriage*, #6 and #8). By having a wedding during Mass, the couple celebrates their spousal love as a reflection of the sacrificial love that the Lord has for the couple and the Church. Also, because the couple about to be married should be worthy to receive the sacrament of marriage fruitfully, the Church recommends that the couple prepare for it by confessing their sins in the sacrament of reconciliation.

The wedding liturgy includes an entrance procession, a greeting, prayers, readings, and a homily. After this, the priest questions the couple concerning their freedom in choosing marriage, their desire to be faithful, and their willingness to have and rear children. The bridal couple then exchanges vows in the presence of the priest, two witnesses, and the assembled Christian community. The groom and bride join hands and in turn verbalize their consent. They promise to be true in good times and bad, in sickness and in health, and to love and honor each other until death. As the Church's official witness, the priest blesses the rings and asks the couple to exchange them as symbols of fidelity and unending love.

The Prayers of the Faithful follow. When marriage takes place within Mass, the Liturgy of the Eucharist proceeds as usual with the nuptial blessing given after the Lord's Prayer. When marriage takes place outside Mass—which should normally be the case when one partner is not Catholic—the nuptial blessing immediately follows the Prayers of the Faithful. The Lord's Prayer and Final Blessing then conclude the liturgy.

When a man and woman exchange their vows, the Church witnesses, blesses, and celebrates their covenantal promises. However, the sacrament of marriage is not just a one-day affair; it unfolds over the years as the husband and wife live out their mutual relationship with each other and the Lord. The risen Lord promises to be with the couple to sustain them on their life's journey. He sanctifies sexual love, a most powerful sign of total, exclusive, intimate sharing. He sustains the couple in the ordinary give-and-take of family life. He empowers them to be signs of love to each other, their children, and to all their friends and acquaintances. Through their daily love and fidelity, they will meet the Lord, who lives within them by the power of the Holy Spirit. The celebration of Christian marriage is "till death do us part."

What Are the Requirements for a Valid Marriage? (CCC, 1625–1631; 1662)

To celebrate the sacrament of marriage validly, the couple must be of mature age, unmarried, and not closely related by blood or marriage. They must also freely consent to marry. Freedom of consent means that neither party is under constraint or impeded by any natural or Church law.

The exchange of consent is the indispensable element that makes the marriage valid. This consent, in which the parties freely give themselves to each other, must be free of coercion or grave external fear. If freedom is lacking, then the marriage never really exists.

Consent means that a couple commits themselves to the lifelong covenant of love into which God has called them. Furthermore, the spouses must be capable of sharing sexually since sexual intercourse is a sign of mutual love and union, the full expression of the mutual love between husband and wife. Finally, the couple must be open to the possibility of raising a family if God blesses the marriage with children.

The ministers of the sacrament of marriage are the bride and bridegroom themselves. Because marriage is an ecclesial reality, Church law requires that a Catholic couple exchange their vows before a priest and two other witnesses. Exchanging vows publicly helps the spouses remain faithful to their commitments.

How Does a Couple Prepare for Marriage? (CCC, 1632–1637)

Marriage is important not only to the couple but to the Church and society as a whole. For this reason, the Church puts a great emphasis on suitable marriage preparations. The witness of loving parents and families is critical, but so are the catechetical efforts of pastors and the parish community.

Preparation for a Christian marriage in most dioceses includes a requirement that the engaged couple participate in a marriage preparation program of some sort. This might take the form of a retreat, a series of workshops, or couple-to-couple meetings. These Church-sponsored programs give the couple an opportunity to learn about what the sacramental commitment entails from members of the community, usually including both couples who are living the sacrament and members of the clergy or lay ecclesial staff of the parish or diocese. During the period of preparation, a priest, deacon, or designated lay ecclesial minister will continue to meet with the couple to prepare them for the serious commitment they are about to make.

When a Catholic marries a non-Catholic Christian (a mixed marriage), special attention is paid to the situation by the couple and those in the parish working with the couple at the various levels of marriage preparation. When a Catholic marries a non-baptized person, an express dispensation must be granted by the bishop for the marriage to be valid. The Catholic partner promises to continue to live his or her Catholic faith and have his or her children baptized and raised in the Catholic faith. The non-Catholic partner is made aware of this pledge but is not required to make any promises. Both partners must know and not exclude the essential purposes and qualities of marriage, and the non-Catholic partner must not exclude the promise of the Catholic partner.

The banns (announcements) of marriage are usually printed in the parish bulletin for three consecutive weeks before the wedding ceremony. The reason for the publication and reading of the banns is to notify the Christian community of the impending celebration and to give informed parties the opportunity to come forward if they know any reason the sacrament of marriage should not take place.

When one of the parties is a non-Catholic, special permission can be obtained from the local bishop and pastor for a minister of another faith to participate in the marriage ceremony. In extraordinary circumstances a dispensation might be given for a minister of another faith to witness the exchange of vows.

What Is an Annulment? (CCC, 1629)

An annulment is an official declaration of the Catholic Church that what appeared to be a valid sacramental marriage in fact was not. A couple may have entered the marriage psychologically immature or lacking true understanding of the demands a marriage covenant makes. One or both partners might not have given free, true consent to the marriage. Perhaps one or both partners intended never to have children. Possibly one or both partners were incapable of sexual relations.

A failed marriage, one that ends in divorce, may never have been a true sacramental marriage to begin with. In this case the couple should submit their situation to the diocesan marriage tribunal (court) for examination and judgment. If it can be shown that the marriage was not valid from the beginning, a declaration of nullity is granted (annulment). The individuals involved are then free to enter a true Christian marriage in the future.

What Are the Principal Effects of the Sacrament of Matrimony? (CCC, 1638–1642)

Christ's love sanctifies the love of husband and wife in the sacrament of marriage. Once the marriage is consummated, an irrevocable, perpetual, and exclusive bond results between the spouses who freely consented to become lifelong partners. Their relationship is covenantal, not simply contractual, in which the Lord showers his graces to perfect their love and strengthen their unity. A major fruit of their life in common is the welcoming of any children God may send them. Their life together, along with their efforts to rear and educate their children in a family setting, is the primary means for a married couple to attain holiness.

What Are the Essential Qualities of a Christian Marriage? (CCC, 1643–1645; 1652–1654; 1664)

Christian marriage involves a total commitment of a couple's bodies, feelings, affections, hearts, wills, and spirits. It results in a deep unity of body, heart, and soul. As a result, marriage demands indissolubility, fidelity, and openness to fertility. Practices contrary to these essential goods include polygamy, which destroys the exclusivity of marriage and undermines the dignity of the man and woman; divorce, which ends up separating what

God has joined together; and refusal of fertility (i.e., artificial contraception or abortion), which deflects marriage from its greatest gift—children.

Married love is a great gift from God. Sexual sharing in a marriage is a profound means of love and commitment between a man and a woman. Its purpose in God's plan is twofold: unitive, that is, to bond a man and woman together as partners for life; and procreative, that is, to share in God's creative activity of bringing new life into the world. Children are the crowning gifts of marriage, contributing to the good of the mother and father. Marriage and the family are the exemplars of God's gift of life and are at the service of life.

Why Is Christian Marriage a Permanent Commitment? (CCC, 1646–1651; 1665)

The example of permanent marriage commitment is a prime way to bring Christ into the world. This is concretely true for the children who result from the marriage. Children first encounter the love and knowledge of God from their parents and are, in fact, living symbols of their parents' love. Children need the stable, reassuring love of a solid marriage to develop healthy attitudes to life and to God.

But a faithful marriage is a powerful sign to those outside of the immediate family as well. Just as God's love is unconditional and eternal, so the Christian husband and wife strive for this ideal in their lives together. Their fidelity and exclusive love is an extraordinary sign to the world of God's fidelity and undying love for his people.

Jesus himself underscored the permanence of the marriage bond:

> He said in reply, "Have you not read that from the beginning the Creator 'made them male and female' and said, 'For this reason a man shall leave his father and mother and be joined to his wife, and the two shall become one flesh'? So they are no longer two, but one flesh. Therefore, what God has joined together, no human being must separate."
>
> —Matthew 19:4–6

Thus the Catholic Church does not permit divorce and remarriage because Jesus forbade it. The covenant made between two validly married Catholics can only be dissolved by the death of one of the partners. In extraordinary circumstances a couple may separate for the good of the children and the individuals involved. Though the civil authority may dissolve the legal aspects of a valid marriage (called in civil law a divorce), the state has no authority to dissolve a true Christian marriage—its true sacramental nature.

According to Church teaching, a legally separated Catholic (divorced under civil law) may not remarry while his or her spouse is alive. This teaching is consistent with the Lord's teaching, "Everyone who divorces his wife and marries another is guilty of adultery" (Lk 16:18). Christ calls his disciples to high standards. Moreover, he gives them the grace to live his commands. The Church encourages a person who is suffering from a broken marriage to continue to celebrate the sacraments, including the reception of communion, and remain close to the Christian community. The Lord promises in a special way to bless those who suffer most. Fellow Christians should support hurting brothers and sisters, pray for them, and help them to "live out their situation in a Christian manner" (CCC, 1649).

A SACRED COVENANT, A HOLY SACRAMENT

Since the close of the Second Vatican Council the Church has placed greater emphasis on marriage as covenant while also re-emphasizing marriage as a sacrament. The first two paragraphs of the Introduction to the *Rite of Marriage* state:

> 1. In virtue of the sacrament of marriage, married Christians signify and share in the mystery of the unity and fruitful love that exists between Christ and his Church; they thus help each other to attain holiness in their married life and in welcoming and rearing children and they have their own special place and gift among the people of God.

> 2. A marriage is established by the marriage covenant, the irrevocable consent that the spouses freely give to and receive from each other. This unique union of a man and a woman and the good of the children impose total fidelity on each of them and the unbreakable unity of their bond.[18]

The notion of a covenant relationship dates back to ancient Israel, before the time of King David. It was a secular term borrowed by the writers of the Jewish scriptures to describe the relationship that God had with his people Israel. In the secular meaning, a covenant was a specific relationship entered into by two unequal parties, usually states. The weaker party sought protection from the more powerful party and agreed to the terms laid out for it by its powerful ally. For its part the more powerful party agreed to offer protection to the weaker party.

The application to the relationship between God and the people, Israel becomes clear when cast in the above light of a covenant relationship. Israel was in need of a protector, as it was often a pawn in the maneuverings of nation-states like Assyria, Babylon, and Egypt. The God of Israel, after the giving of the Ten Commandments, became Israel's protector and promised to always be faithful to the people of Israel. For its part, Israel agreed to abide by the commandments outlined in the Decalogue.

As the history of Israel unfolded, later prophets would emphasize the relational aspect of the covenant between Israel and her God. It was a natural development to compare God's love for his people to that of a bridegroom for his bride. God was said to have "nuptial" love for his people.

In the New Covenant inaugurated by Jesus, the image of a wedding looms large as a symbol of God's love for his people. Jesus' presence and actions at the wedding feast at Cana (Jn 2:1–11) establish the sacramental quality of marriage. This event also expands the image of the wedding feast, promoted by the prophets, as a foretelling of the messianic banquet.

In speaking of marriage the *Catechism of the Catholic Church* talks about the "spousal love" between Christ and the Church.[19] Marriage as a sacrament points toward the love between Christ and the Church and offers the grace to make present his love in the concrete ways that the two married people live their life together. We say that sacraments are efficacious signs, meaning that they bring about what is signified or pointed to. If marriage points toward the hidden reality of Christ's love for the Church, then in a Christian marriage the couple creates that same love in their own personal way.

There is another important but less obvious point to be made about the covenant relationship of marriage. That is that the two married people, in taking on the responsibility to be a sign of Christ's love for the Church, willingly bring about an irrevocable, permanent bond. This is because their very commitment points toward the unfailingly permanent love of God, and because a sacrament brings about what it signifies, the bond entered into by two married people creates the same type of bond as the bond between God and his people: permanent and lasting.

There is a bit of a contradiction here that has to do with the fact that we experience ourselves as sinners called to holiness. It is this: how can two people, with all of their inadequacies and frailties, dare to call into existence a bond that is like that between God and his people, and one that is permanent and lasting? Can any of us guarantee fidelity like that which God has for his people? We would be fools if we said we could. In raising marriage to a sacramental level it would seem that Jesus is asking perhaps too much of a married couple.

The answer to this dilemma is to be found in the original notion of a covenant relationship. Israel was the weaker, sinful party to the covenant with God. God knew that Israel as a nation would flounder and wander away yet continued to renew the covenant with Israel again and again. Because it was a permanent bond, the relationship was, and is, permanent. In other words, no matter what Israel did to harm the covenant, it was God who was always faithful, always calling Israel to a deeper holiness.

The same is true for the sacrament of marriage. In a sense, the two people who marry each other represent, or symbolize, the Church and the entire people of God. The two people making their vows together can be said to represent Israel before Mount Sinai, ready to receive their terms of the covenant, the Ten Commandments. In other words, marriage as a sacrament is not a solitary act between two people. Rather, a sacramental marriage in the Catholic Church begins when two baptized Christians make vows together in the presence of a minister of the Church. The ecclesial community, which also includes relatives, friends, and acquaintances, gives acceptance of, and witness to, a new social unit, which is the foundation of family life within the Christian community. Not only does marriage spring from the community, it creates it as well. With the arrival of children, the Christian family becomes the Church on the most local level.

The other notion to ponder is the fact that just as the Church is made up of sinners called to holiness, so the two newly married spouses embark on a journey of holiness where they will be called to confront the harmful aspects of their own sinfulness. This journey is a journey toward holiness and wholeness. Just as God knew beforehand that Israel could fail its part of the covenant, yet was always present and faithful to Israel, we too can trust that God will be faithful to two people who could falter in their permanent bond by their fallible conduct.

In the end, perhaps the most important thing about the aspect of covenant is that it speaks of an ongoing, lasting relationship between God and the two married people. Placing the emphasis on relationship calls for a more dynamic process that moves beyond the legalities of civil and Church laws to a relationship that relies on the living, loving God to sustain the core of the couple's commitment.

A BRIEF HISTORY OF THE MARRIAGE RITE

In the first century, marriage rites presumably followed Jewish and pagan customs, with the elimination of anything that was explicitly objectionable to Christians. The majority of marriages took place in the home and were private celebrations that did not require the presence of Church leaders. Both families publicly agreed upon a marriage contract. The groom and the veiled bride were brought together and blessed, and then everyone feasted. Usually a family member, often the bride's father, prayed the blessing. Late in the first century Ignatius, the bishop of Antioch, said that it was better if Christians married with the approval of the local bishop so that "their marriage may be according to the Lord, and not after their own lust." He did not, however, suggest any particular ritual for a Christian marriage.

Over the next few centuries certain specifically Christian customs developed for weddings. The marriage blessing began to take on a definite liturgical structure, and there was an increasing reluctance to marry during Advent or Lent. In some places a celebration of the Eucharist followed the blessing of the couple, and on occasion the Eucharist actually replaced the traditional wedding feast.

The primary image of marriage through the first millennium was that of a contract. In the Middle Ages the porch of the church became the place where legal contracts were ratified before God and before the community; therefore, marriages gradually moved from the home to the porch of the church. The pressure to have marriages take place in the church grew stronger as the need grew for written documentation to prove legitimate births and the right of inheritance. Priests were the only people in most villages who could read and write; therefore, it became necessary to have them present at the wedding. It was only around the sixteenth century that all marriages moved into the church and that the celebration of a Nuptial Mass became the norm.

Wedding vows had to be pronounced both freely and in public. Thus they became the first liturgical texts in the language of the people rather than in Latin. Wedding vows themselves have changed very little over the centuries. The *Use of York,* a liturgical manual written in the fourteenth century, contains the following vow:

> Here I take you [name] to my wedded wife, to hold
> and to have at bed and at board, for fairer for foul-
> er, for better for worse, in sickness and in health, till
> death us do part, if holy Church it will ordain, and
> thereto I plight you my troth.

One of the major changes in the wedding ceremony since Vatican II has been the stress on the equality of the marriage partners. The pre–Vatican II rite included a prayer for the bride that she be "faithful to one embrace . . . honorable in her chastity." There was no similar prayer for the groom. The post–Vatican II rite contains no such inequalities.

4

Special Pastoral Issues

INTERFAITH AND MIXED MARRIAGES

Recent statistics indicate that about 40 percent of American Catholics marry someone from a different religious affiliation.[20] What this means for those conducting a marriage prep program is that traditional and familiar religious language and concepts cannot be presumed.

Religious differences can also be a source of conflict in a marriage, especially if the question of the religious upbringing of children is unresolved.[21] Thus, it behooves the couple to discuss openly their expectations concerning how it is they will resolve this potential source of tension.

The influence of the marriage prep program in assisting engaged couples to think through the differences in their religious views and/or practices is often quite significant. Lead couples and team members can go a long way toward modeling acceptance of differences and enthusiasm for making spirituality a significant aspect of the early marriage commitment.

When working with a couple in this situation keep in mind the following:

1. Don't apologize for your own faith.

A person from another religious tradition might come to the sessions with a mixture of curiosity and indifference. If he or she witnesses team members and lead couples downplaying their own Catholic experience, then this person could form the impression that Catholicism is not very important.

2. Don't oversell the Catholic experience either.

Know your faith and be comfortable in expressing how it "works" for you by solving the bigger problems of meaning and belonging in your life. Keep in mind that you are modeling a certain way of being religious even though you might not be intentional about it.

3. Be ready to give good reasons why anyone might be interested in exploring Catholicism.

A marriage prep program can be looked at as another way of evangelizing, that is, bringing the good news to people. If there are any inquiries about the Catholic Church, be ready to refer the couple to the local parish's catechumenate program. A young couple that participates in this type of program receives, in many respects, the best form of preparation for marriage.

4. Without trying to scare the couple, be ready to discuss with them the facts of marriages between people of different backgrounds.

Research has shown that in 50 percent of these marriages one spouse converts to the other's religion; that the mother has a stronger influence on the children's religious identification, but that the father's participation is important for the religious development of sons; and that there is a slightly higher divorce rate in marriages between people of different religious affiliations.[22]

5. Regardless of the question of where the two will worship, stress with the couple the importance of developing a spirituality of marriage.

This involves, in part, an attitude that our lives are interconnected in a web of communities, that all humans share a common bond, and that a transcendent force is somehow at work in the cosmos and in our lives. Ask the couple to seriously consider how it is they intend to celebrate and ritualize the important aspects of their lives, and whether religion and spirituality have any place in that task. For example, talk with them about which holidays they will celebrate and how, how they will mark births and deaths, and how they will respond to life's crises like a serious illness or accident.

COHABITATION

Engaged couples living together before marriage present a unique and significant pastoral challenge to anyone involved in the ministry of marriage preparation. About 50 percent of couples seeking marriage in the Church are already living together under one roof.

The National Conference of Catholic Bishops defines cohabitation as a couple who have been living together at least four nights a week for an extended period of time, where a commitment to each other exists, and where there is some recognition that the couple form a family or household.[23] Many people do not use the term "cohabitation" but use the term "living together" to describe a situation where there is a commitment to share economic and household resources, and where the commitment includes a serious level of emotional and sexual sharing.

In the culture of the 1960s, the attitude toward premarital sex and cohabitation was rather carefree. If it wasn't "harmful," an action was deemed permissible, and many people in authority positions outside the Church saw no harm in the choice of a couple to live together before marriage. The Church, of course, did not share this view.

Although many in our culture understand and agree with the Church's teaching on the immorality of sexual intercourse before marriage, this teaching is far from clear to all. Because it is clearly countercultural, many find it difficult to embrace. Yet the Church holds firm to its teaching. The *Catechism of the Catholic Church* states that sex outside marriage is "gravely contrary to the dignity of persons and of human sexuality which is naturally ordered to the good of spouses and the generation and education of children" (*CCC*, 2353).

In addition to the Church's convictions, we also have the benefit of a generation of research on the effects of cohabitation. Longitudinal statistical pools of information suggest that divorce rates among couples who lived together before marriage are higher than among couples who did not live together. The reasons for this appear to be found in the very teaching on marriage that the Church has been expounding throughout its long history.

Put succinctly, a lasting marriage commitment requires a mature freedom where a person can speak honestly and forthrightly with his or her partner about the concerns and tensions of the day. Anything that limits this freedom places hidden "strings" on the relationship that implicitly state: "If you raise this issue I might not stick around." The foundational issues, because they have the greatest potential for conflict, often do not get the attention they deserve. One study found that couples who lived together tended to avoid issues such as finances, careers, children, and the like because of the potential negative impact on the relationship.[24]

Thus we can see that cohabitation can actually cause harm to the marriage bond down the line, especially if a deep trust and confidence in the permanence of the relationship has not been formed. A marriage built on withholding of trust and self-surrender does not live up to the ideals of Christ put forth by the Church. There is good reason to be concerned about a couple who lives together.

A Pastoral Approach to Cohabitation

As in any pastoral dilemma the person of Jesus needs to be central in finding appropriate solutions. We can turn here to the story "The Woman at the Well" (Jn 4:4–42) for developing an approach that can be helpful. In this story we find Jesus meeting a Samaritan woman at Jacob's well. The two engage in a dialogue that sometimes appears to be a sparring match. At one point Jesus tells the woman to "go call your husband and come back" (Jn 4:16). When she replies that she doesn't have a husband, Jesus confronts her honestly and tells her that she is correct, that she has had five previous husbands, and that the man she is living with now is not her husband. As she becomes aware that this is a man she cannot manipulate, this confrontation becomes the beginning of a deeper conversion for the woman.

Thus, we find that Jesus focuses on being honest about what is happening and on conversion. These two points can become the central strategy for anyone working with preparing an engaged couple for marriage.

Honesty and Conversion

It does no good for anyone to deny that a couple is living together. The most likely reason for an engaged couple to deny this is fear that they will be refused marriage. This sometimes leads them to a deception of the priest, deacon, or lay minister doing initial preparation work with them. Most seasoned priests, deacons, and pastoral ministers know from experience that moving the couple beyond fear of judgment and rejection leads to a much deeper dialogue about the consequences of cohabitation. Only with such a dialogue, guided by God's grace, can the couple be led to carefully reconsider their situation.

Most dioceses have a set of policies and procedures concerning the issue of cohabitation about which the priest, deacon, or pastoral minister of the parish should know. The lead couple or team member who encounters the issue should start first at the parish in which the wedding will take place, in discovering what approach to take. In many cases the priest, deacon, or pastoral minister has already become aware of a couple's cohabitation.

More than likely, if any action should be taken, the priest, deacon, or lay ecclesial minister working with the couple should do it.

What about the issue of cohabitation when it surfaces in the marriage prep program itself? Here again, the issue is one of honesty, which can lead to the deepening of conversion. The following points may help the lead couple or team members in developing an approach toward this issue.

1. Remember your role as a lead couple or team member when this issue surfaces. If a couple confides in you concerning their living situation, it is because they trust you and believe that you will maintain confidentiality. Your primary role is to be a mentor, guide, facilitator, and then teacher. As such, respecting the confidentiality of the engaged couple is important. Before you work with an engaged couple, it is a good idea to ask your pastor how the issue of cohabitation will be treated and what your role is regarding this specific issue. By respecting the confidentiality of the couple you can do much to dialogue with them concerning their experiences and the stance of the Church (see below, #3).

   Keep in mind that the priest, deacon, or lay ecclesial minister usually has several meetings with an engaged couple before the couple begins a marriage prep program. Chances are this minister is already aware that a couple is living together and has already taken steps to address the situation. You may or may not have access to this bit of information. It is not your role to ask a couple to make different living arrangements. This is the role of the pastoral staff person, and it is his or her responsibility to decide how to approach this pastoral situation.

2. If you are uncomfortable working with an engaged couple that is living together, you should discuss this with your parish priest as part of your training. You need to be informed about the diocesan policies concerning cohabitation and how they are implemented in your local parish. Before you decide to discontinue working with an engaged couple because you object to the morality of their action, consider that you run the risk of violating the original hospitality that you offered the couple when you began working with them. Consider making this hospitality an evangelical hospitality by continuing to work with them and calling them to a deeper truth at the same time.

3. Above all else, it is incumbent on the lead couple or team members to "teach as the Church teaches." In discussing some of the reasons why couples live together before marriage Pope John Paul II concludes:

> Each of these elements presents the Church with arduous pastoral problems, by reason of the serious consequences deriving from them, both religious and moral (the loss of the religious sense of marriage seen in the light of the covenant of God with his people; deprivation of the grace of the sacrament; grave scandal) and also social consequences (the destruction of the concept of the family; the weakening of the sense of fidelity, also toward society; possible psychological damage to the children; strengthening of selfishness).
>
> The pastors and the ecclesial community should take care to become acquainted with such situations and their actual causes, case by case. They should make tactful and respectful contact with the couples concerned and enlighten them patiently, correct them charitably, and show them the witness of Christian family life in such a way as to smooth the path for them to regularize their situation.[25]

Thus, the lead couple or team members need to avoid condoning the behavior yet also avoid judging the engaged couple so harshly that it drives them away from the community. The most important element that Christian married couples have to offer a couple who is living together is the dual witness of a public commitment and the virtue of joy that flows from the grace of a marriage that was sacramentalized in a public way.

4. A respectful listening to the engaged couple's experience and a charitable challenge to try something different seem to be what Pope John Paul II is calling for in the above statement. There are many different reasons why a couple might choose to live together. Listening to these reasons can easily signal respect. Respectful listening can be combined with good, solid reasons why living apart until the marriage occurs could be an invitation to a deepening of maturity on the part of the engaged couple.

5. Keep in mind that the grace of God works in ways that we often cannot see or comprehend. While a couple living together presents a pastoral

difficulty, it is also an opportunity for evangelization. The witness of a married couple to an engaged couple living together plants seeds of faith and maturity that may take years to grow into fullness. We often touch people in unseen ways. That is the legacy of faith and grace.

DEALING WITH RESISTANCE

From time to time a lead couple or team member will encounter an individual or a couple or who resists the process and makes it clear that one or both do not want to participate in the marriage prep program. Some behaviors that indicate that there might be resistance are:

- Extended silences, especially after attempts to involve the party have been made by a lead couple or team member

- Frequently passing when it is his or her turn to share

- Consistently answering questions in short, terse sentences

- Letting the fiancé answer for him or her

- Clear verbal challenges to having to participate in the program

- Disinterested body posture such as rolling the eyes, looking away, sighing, and foot jiggling

- Talking to someone else during presentations or simply not doing the exercises requested

What to Do

In most cases resistance can be overcome by directly addressing the behaviors noticed as soon as possible. It is best not to let such behaviors go on too long, as they can become entrenched and begin affecting the participation of other members (if it is a group program) or engender anger on the part of the lead couple or other team members.

Reasons for resistance vary with each couple. The lead couple or team member might want to begin thinking about the following areas when getting ready to address the issue:

- Possible conflict between the couple and the priest, deacon, or lay minister preparing them for marriage at the local parish level. Sometimes this preparation does not go well, and the couple comes into the sessions angry and expecting the trouble to continue.

- Possible conflict between the two engaged people either as a result of relationship difficulties or as a result of an issue raised by the priest, deacon, or pastoral minister at the local parish level.

- A conflict that arises at the beginning of the marriage prep program. Sometimes personality conflicts begin to emerge where one or both of the engaged parties reacts negatively to either a lead couple or team member. Sometimes there is resistance because a couple does not understand what is expected of them throughout the program.

The more quickly action is taken, the more quickly the facilitation of the session gets back on track. It is up to the lead couple or team member to make the unconscious resistance conscious so that it can be dealt with adequately. Here are a few suggestions to help you deal with resistance.

1. In the beginning of the program, whether it be a group program or a couple-to-couple program, someone can address the possibility of resistance by saying: "We don't expect you to like everything we do over the course of the program; indeed, you might even have negative reactions to some of the exercises. That's okay. We do want you to be as open as possible to sharing your experiences and reflecting more deeply on your commitment to one another. Also, in your preparation so far you all have had interaction with someone on the pastoral staff at your parish. By now you most probably have met with the priest, deacon, or lay minister who is guiding your marriage preparation process and perhaps even the music director, liturgist, or wedding coordinator. In our experience, most of these encounters go well; sometimes, however, there are glitches or conflicts over different things that can make some people feel negative. If this has happened to you, we want you to be able to talk about this when appropriate, especially if it prevents you from participating fully in this program."

2. Once the program has begun and there is still resistance, the best thing is to ask the couple or individual to speak to a team member privately. In the case of a couple-to-couple program this invitation can occur naturally in the room where you usually meet. Keep the focus on the behaviors observed and keep your conclusions tentative. An example might be:

"Michael, I noticed that you've been quite silent for this entire session. Is something on your mind that's stopping you from participating?" Allow the individual to say what he or she is thinking and feeling.

3. If an individual mentions conflict with the priest, deacon, or lay minister or the music director, liturgist, or wedding coordinator, try to empathize with him or her by validating the feelings and frustrations. Resist the urge to defend the minister. Your job is to reduce resistance, not to defend the person or the policy. On the other hand, it is appropriate to offer assistance in problem solving, especially if the couple feels frustrated with the person who is working with them. The best thing to do in most cases is to encourage the couple to talk honestly with the person with whom they are having conflict.

ENCOURAGING THE SILENT PARTNER, WORKING WITH THE TALKATIVE PARTNER

Whether your program is designed around a couple-to-couple or group format you will encounter from time to time an individual who is much more silent than his or her partner. In cases such as this it is important to assess whether the silence is due to resistance or is more part of the temperament of the individual. One must keep in mind that there is a wide range of relationship styles and that just because a person or couple act and respond differently than you would doesn't necessarily signal a problem. Some people simply prefer not to speak as much as others and will resent any attempt to make them share at a pace at which they are uncomfortable.

Silence rooted in resistance is a different issue from silence that is rooted in one's temperament and personality. In the case of resistance, once the problem is addressed and cleared up, the person usually begins to participate more.

Silence That Signals a More Serious Problem

There is another type of silence that might signal a more serious difficulty, and that is a silence that indicates an individual's passivity in relationship with a partner's apparent dominance or control. Cases such as this often manifest themselves in an "over-adequate/under-adequate" pattern, where one person often speaks, interprets, and acts for the other more silent, passive person. Another characteristic of this pattern is a clear lack of confidence on the part of the quiet partner and a clear confidence and competence on the part of the talkative partner. This type of pattern becomes evident, for instance, when one person is asked a direct question but his or her fiancé answers. Another manifestation of this pattern is when one person always takes the lead in answering and the other person holds back, gives simple yes/no responses, or clearly defers to his or her fiancé.

An over-adequate/under-adequate relationship pattern could signal problems later in the life of the relationship. As anyone in a long-term marriage knows, we change and mature as the years go by, and anything that is unfinished, rigid, or unhealthy about our relationship will eventually have to be dealt with. Therapists commonly work with couples in which one party is asking for major changes, moving from an "over-under" pattern of relating to more of an "equal-equal" pattern. The latter offers far more equality in the sharing of tasks, verbalization of desires, and assertion of needs.

Clearly, an over-adequate/under-adequate relationship will raise questions for a lead couple or team member. The most important type of response is a gentle but firm intervention that simply reflects back to the couple the behaviors observed. It is important to let the couple know that you have observed specific behaviors without attaching interpretations of good or bad on these behaviors. Also, you can frame the intervention in a way that roots it in your experience. Thus, an intervention might go something like this: "We noticed that in the last session you, Bob, did most of the talking for Sally. In our experience, marriage requires a lot of sharing on the part of both people, and we're a bit concerned that we're not seeing a lot of that. Sally, is there a reason that you let Bob speak for you so much last time?"

Once the issue is confronted and put out in the open, many engaged couples will at least appreciate that the concern was expressed. Many others will directly address the issues raised, as they also want to ensure success in their relationship. Some, however, will become defensive and only acknowledge a small part of the problem. It is best not to get into a control struggle with them, as your role is to help them prepare for, not prevent them from, marriage. If you feel that the problem is a serious one, you can suggest that the couple talks to the priest, deacon, or LEM who is working with them at the parish. You also can make a referral to a therapist who is experienced in relationship counseling. This is especially helpful when a couple acknowledges that they have been experiencing problems with this crucial part of their growing relationship.

What to Do With the Talker

Sometimes one party is not necessarily dominant, but he or she is simply talkative. This often occurs with people who are very extroverted (they talk in order to think through information) or who have low self-esteem. Talking, or getting connected with others, is a major way for a person such as this to receive feedback and feel okay about himself or herself. This person might not have a highly developed sense of how he or she is perceived by the group and can often benefit from encouragement and gentle challenge.

Effective encouragement centers on making it clear to everyone involved that all opinions count and that everyone is invited to share at least once per exercise. Gentle challenge is needed when the talker breaks the rules and interrupts or intrudes. The leader of the exercise must gently and firmly remind that person that it is not his or her turn yet or that others still need to share. This can be done with humor, especially if trust has developed. Also, it can be said in a way that creates affirmation for the talker as well as others in the group. An example of this could be, "Ken, you have a lot of good things to say, but we also need to hear from the rest of the group (or from your fiancé)."

In summary, the lead couple or team members should keep in mind the following when dealing with a silent or overly talkative participant:

1. When you begin any session or exercise, emphasize the rule that you want each person to share his or her response to at least one of the questions or items contained in the exercise.

2. Early on, set the norm for conversation using the "Rules for Simple Sharing." (See pp. 70–71.)

3. When you encounter a person who is silent, make an assessment as to whether the silence is rooted in resistance, personal temperament, or a relationship pattern such as the over-adequate/under-adequate pattern.

4. In all cases, develop trust and rapport with the silent participant. If the silence is rooted in resistance, get at the core of it by being honest with the person and asking for an honest response back. If the silence is rooted in temperament, signal acceptance and confidence that this person can communicate his or her needs when necessary.

5. If you determine that the silence is rooted in an over-adequate/under-adequate relationship pattern, then prepare to raise this issue with the

couple. If this is a group program, it is important that this confrontation take place away from the group so that confidentiality can be maintained. If you need help in preparing for such an intervention, ask someone you trust and who is competent in handling such cases how you might proceed.

6. In dealing with the talkative partner remember to set the norms for sharing early and often. The best remedy in this situation is for the lead couple or team members to set the pace and intervene as soon as the "talker" begins to interrupt or talks too long.

CONFIDENTIALITY

When an engaged couple comes to a marriage prep program, most are not concerned with whether the material they discuss will be kept confidential. Yet once they become aware of the issue, most engaged couples will expect that what they say will not be reported back to a parish priest, deacon, or pastoral minister. Thus, we can speak of a general expectation for confidentiality of matters discussed in both the group program and lead couple format.

Many parishes give a lead couple or team members for a group program basic information about the engaged couple. This information may be as basic as street addresses and phone numbers. In a couple-to-couple program the priest, deacon, or lay minister is much more free to discuss with the lead couple information of a more serious nature. For example, a minister might discuss with a lead couple whether a couple is living together and what has been done to challenge this situation. In other cases, special information that is pertinent to the participation in the program might be revealed to the lead couple.

In the case of a group program there is usually little sharing of personal information about the couple. There is often, however, some sharing on the part of the group program leaders back to the parish concerning attendance in the program.

It is important for program leaders and team members to establish right away with the engaged couple how the flow of information back to the priest, deacon, or lay minister is going to work. This means that some simple rules need to be worked out between the parish and the people administering the direct service of marriage preparation.

Generally speaking, the more confidentiality can be established and maintained, the more trust can be expected to develop; it follows that with greater trust comes greater participation and ownership of the program. Thus, guaranteeing confidentiality—that a program team member or lead couple won't secretly report back to the priest, deacon, or pastoral minister—is a good thing to do.

The following are some simple steps that a lead couple or team members can follow in establishing the norm of confidentiality:

1. Early in the first session establish the expectations for confidentiality. Say something like this: "It is our expectation that what is said in these sessions is confidential in nature; we do not report back to whoever is working with you at the parish. If you have a specific difficulty that involves your priest, deacon, or lay minister, we will listen to you and help you find a resolution to the problem. We won't get involved in any difficulty unless asked, and even then we might decline to get involved."

2. Establish how you will act if a serious problem emerges. You might want to say something like this to the couple(s): "Sometimes a serious issue beyond the normal issues or problems emerges. If this occurs, and we feel that it is a serious threat to your relationship, we will speak with you first about the matter. We might encourage you to speak with whoever is working with you at the parish, and if you agree to do so, then the matter at our level might be resolved. If we feel that we must speak to whoever is preparing you, we will talk to you first. This type of situation is a very rare occurrence. We want to establish the expectations for confidentiality right off the bat so that there are no surprises down the line."

As with any relationship, establishing expectations and trust is very important. A couple who feels they know what to expect and can trust you to keep your word will relax and begin to own the goals of the program. It is important to be clear with the couple(s) about how it is you will act if a serious problem emerges. A couple who trusts that you will encourage them to first handle the problem themselves will feel that you are treating them like adults.

When Is It Permissible to Break Confidentiality?

There are some difficulties that emerge where a lead couple or team members might feel bound by conscience to speak to the priest, deacon, or lay minister, even after saying something to the couple. These issues represent serious difficulties in the relationship and can be generally characterized by the following:

1. An Indication of Serious and Active Substance Abuse

All of us know that substance abuse is a serious problem in our society, and we shouldn't be surprised when an engaged couple manifests a problem in this area. Because of the tendency toward denial over this issue, it is sometimes hard to detect a problem even when there is an active and quite serious difficulty. A person who is dependent on alcohol or another substance can easily mask the dependency or simply deny that there is a problem. He or she can show up at a program sober, for example, yet maintain a dependency by drinking heavily at other times.

Sometimes a problem of this sort surfaces during the marriage prep program, and then the lead couple or team members are left with a dilemma concerning whether to speak to the engaged couple. Even though these types of confrontations are difficult, it is always best to err on the side of honesty. Simply saying, "N. we have become concerned that you might have a problem with . . ." is a sufficient intervention to get the ball rolling. Also mention that you intend to speak to the appropriate person on the parish staff. Any intervention like this should be done with the idea in mind of moving the person or couple into counseling as soon as possible so that the issue can be addressed quickly.

2. Physical and/or Psychological Abuse

This situation emerges in a public way very infrequently. The most likely people to see the first hints of abuse of this sort will be doctors and other medical providers. A woman coming in for her annual checkup might confide in her doctor that she is in an abusive relationship with her fiancé. But this is an often hidden issue, and is hidden from Church representatives very well, because of the shame, the embarrassment, and perhaps the threat of physical harm that is associated with the problem.

Nevertheless, it sometimes emerges in a marriage prep program that there is physical abuse present in a couple's relationship. If this does, it is important to construct a strategy carefully. Protection of the person being abused should be the first concern. Some abusers will retaliate against their victims if the victims attempt to break free. The case of physical abuse is one where it seems permissible for a lead couple or team members to discuss their concerns directly with the priest, deacon, or pastoral minister, even before saying anything to the couple. In fact, it might be best not to say anything until a strategy is constructed that maximizes the best possible solution for the couple to get help.

One strategy, after discussing this with the priest, deacon, or pastoral minister, is for that person to speak privately with the victim of abuse and raise the issue with her (in most cases the victim of physical abuse is the woman). The support of the Church can be offered as well as a clear statement that the Church in no way condones an abusive relationship. If information about safe shelters needs to be given out, that can be done at this time. This strategy allows the priest, deacon, or pastoral minister to assess the relative safety of a person involved in such a relationship.

Once safety can be assured, the priest, deacon, or pastoral minister is in a position to confront the behavior directly and make a referral to counseling. Many men who become physically abusive have themselves been abused, and as long as there is not a pattern of substance abuse present, they can be helped in controlling and managing their anger so that the violence is extinguished completely. Certainly, a referral for counseling is in order in this case, and the couple will need to postpone the wedding until the problem is resolved.

It sometimes happens that the issue is one of emotional abuse: the presence of put-downs, belittling comments, criticism, and anger directed toward the other person that clearly suppresses his or her self-esteem and spells trouble down the line. In this case, the lead couple or team members have much more freedom to address this directly to the couple by pointing out the behavior and how it appears to be affecting the relationship. Again, stating that you will need to contact the priest, deacon, or lay minister working with the couple at the parish, if the pattern is seriously harmful, is a strategy that says to the couple that there are certain behaviors that are certain to kill a relationship and may even prevent a sacramental bond from being established in the first place.

In all of the strategies outlined above the main goal is not to punish or embarrass but to raise hope that a better relationship is possible if the couple is able to confront the harmful behavior and willing to seek professional help. While such a confrontation is seldom pleasant, it serves as a witness of honesty and truthfulness that the Church will not deny real problems when they surface.

THE ISSUE OF A UNITY CANDLE

At first glance it would seem that a topic such as the unity candle should not be part of a marriage preparation manual. After all, the topic of the unity candle belongs more properly to the details of planning for the actual wedding ceremony. But because it remains a contentious issue in some places, it is quite possible that the engaged couple will raise this issue.

The unity candle is a relatively recent phenomenon, having been added to some Catholic weddings in the last thirty years or so. It is not an official part of the Catholic *Rite of Marriage*, and many dioceses restrict or prohibit the use of the unity candle during the actual wedding ceremony. This, of course, often causes frustration in the couple preparing for marriage, especially if they had plans to use the candle or if one partner belongs to a faith community where it is commonly used.

Some unity candles are shaped in such a way that there are three distinct wicks. Two of the wicks are on the periphery of the candle and are lit before the ceremony begins. Sometime after the exchange of consent (vows) the couple goes to the unity candle, and each lights a taper from one of the already-lit wicks. Together they light the middle wick, symbolizing the new unity of the "two become one." Other times, three separate candles are used. Two tapers are lit before the liturgy, and as above, after the exchange of consent husband and wife together light the larger candle in the center.

The reason that some parishes and dioceses do not permit the unity candle to be used has to do with the potential confusion of what liturgical action constitutes a sacramental marriage. The Church teaches that since the exchange of consent is the fundamental liturgical action (in other words it's what makes a marriage a marriage), no other ritual action should compete with or, as sometimes happens, overshadow it. The unity candle or something like a prolonged exchange of the Sign of Peace may begin to dominate and overshadow the liturgical action of the exchange of consent in which a man and woman vow to form a unity of the whole of life. Often when it comes to ritualizing our most sacred moments, less is truly more.

That is why the liturgical guidelines call for the sacraments to be celebrated with a noble simplicity.

Others, of course, feel that the above objections do not hold much sway and that the unity candle is a relatively harmless addition to the liturgy that further symbolizes the notion of the "two become one." Without taking a stand as to what is right or wrong, it is important for the lead couple or team members to be aware that this might be a potential area of conflict between the engaged couple and the parish. While it may appear to be a small thing, it is usually the "small things" that explode to create large conflicts.

Just serving as a listening and friendly ear can go a long way in helping diffuse any anger and tension over an issue such as this. Be careful, however, not to serve as an intermediary for the couple, since your role is not defined this way. You can listen sympathetically and offer suggestions that encourage the couple to either accept the situation or talk again to the parish representative about liturgical guidelines. In some cases you may be able to help the couple understand the reasons behind such a decision. Whatever the outcome, this may be a valuable opportunity for the couple to hear clearly, and for the first time, the theology of marriage that emphasizes their role as serving as ministers of the sacrament by speaking their vows publicly. If nothing else, the couple may at least feel a deeper pride at knowing that marriage is the only sacrament where the ministers of the sacrament are the two people receiving it.

Sometimes couples resolve any conflict on this issue between their personal desires and the liturgical traditions of the Church by lighting the unity candle as part of a simple meal prayer at the reception. This is a nice way to signal that the wedding feast can begin.

5

Techniques That Enhance Sharing

The following techniques are presented with the understanding that the lead couple or team leader may already possess a great deal of knowledge and experience concerning how to facilitate sharing between people. These techniques should be taken for what they are: techniques. In reality it is the leadership of the lead couple or marriage preparation team that is most responsible for meaningful sharing. Your energy, enthusiasm, and willingness to assist in the preparation of an engaged couple for marriage are in themselves helpful in facilitating dialogue. The following techniques are meant to compliment the accumulated experience and wisdom that you bring to the task of facilitating preparation.

The Good and New

Desired Outcome: Beginning a session that emphasizes the positive in people's lives while allowing everyone a chance to share.

Best Used: In the beginning of a session to gather the group.

"The Good and New" is an exercise that can be done with two to ten couples, depending on the time available.[26] The goal of the exercise is to build rapport and a positive mindset among participants. This exercise is meant to be done quickly, with little comment from participants.

Have each person in the group say one thing that has been "good and new" for him or her since the last time the group met. It is best to simply move around the circle, giving each person ten to twenty seconds to tell the group his or her "good and new." Of course, as with any exercise, if a person does not wish to participate he or she can simply say, "pass."

Sharing of Personal Symbols

Desired Outcome: Deepening of trust and sharing within a group based on the sharing of personal symbols. This exercise often facilitates in-depth sharing of personal stories.

Best Used: After the group has achieved some cohesiveness and when people feel more trust in the group, usually around the third or fourth session of any process. It can also be used at the beginning of any couple-to-couple session. This exercise can also be used at the last session to bring the entire program to a close.

"Sharing of Personal Symbols" is an exercise where people are asked to bring with them a personal memento that has given meaning to their lives. The setting for this exercise can be informal or ritualized. In an informal setting people sit in a circle and simply take turns explaining to the group the meaning of their symbols. In a ritualized setting there may be a quiet time for music and then a time for people to light individual votive candles, place them on a table or altar, then speak about the personal meaning of their symbols.

If comments are given when people share their symbols, they should be affirming and positive. Some examples of symbols that may be shared are pictures, engagement rings, and jewelry given by parents or grandparents, poems, photographs, and memorabilia from an important time in one's life.

This exercise easily can be adapted during the session on children by having everyone bring one or two photos from his or her own family of origin. Then, to begin the session, participants share their photos, telling stories from their own experience. In a group program, couples should break up into small groups for sharing. In a couple-to-couple program, the sharing takes place between the lead couple and the engaged couple.

The Whip Around

Desired Outcome: Checking in with what people are thinking or feeling about a given session; allowing people to give feedback quickly and succinctly.

Best Used: At the end of a session to do a quick evaluation and/or to assess the impact of the session on a person. Sometimes used after a more serious discussion, or where there is a lot of silence that is confusing to the facilitator.

"The Whip Around" allows the group to give feedback on a specific question that is given to them by the facilitator or team. The benefit of this exercise is that it allows everyone in the group either to say how he or she was affected by the session or to give specific feedback on a particular question. It is always best to have the question in mind that will be asked of the group. The facilitator poses the questions and then tells the group that they will "whip around" the circle and give each person about twenty seconds to respond to the question. Remember, as in all group exercises, individuals must be given the option of passing. In the case of a marriage prep group, whether it is a large group or a just a lead couple and engaged couple, some of the questions can be phrased this way:

- As a result of this session, one thing I will either work on or be aware of this week is . . .

- One thing that I learned about myself tonight is . . .

- One thing that I learned about my fiancé is . . .

The Group Within a Group

Desired Outcome: Enhancement of listening by a large group, especially where there is increased tension and/or stereotypes that need to be challenged without creating animosity.

Best Used: When there is a need to allow certain opinions and feelings to surface without being challenged immediately. This exercise will take from forty minutes to an hour.

"The Group Within a Group" is a good technique to use in a group of between twenty to fifty members. It consists of having an outer ring and an inner ring. The group can either stand or sit depending on the length of the exercise. In a group of around twenty people there might be six people in the inner circle and fourteen in the outer circle. One way to use this exercise in a marriage prep setting is to have a representative group of women sit or stand in the inner circle. They are told to begin a discussion among themselves about a specific topic. For instance, they might be asked what they want to see happen when they have conflict with their fiancés. Each member of the inner group is told that when she has spoken her mind that she should go to the outer ring. Other women from the outer ring, when ready to speak, come into the circle and say what they are thinking. No one on the outer circle is allowed to comment.

After a period of time the facilitator asks if there are any more women in the outer circle who want to share. If not, then a representative group of men are asked to go into the inner circle, and they are asked to respond to the same question. The process goes on until every man who wants to share has been given an opportunity to share. Then, the circles are joined into one big circle, and there is processing of what people heard—the commonalities shared between men and women and the differences.

Rules for Simple Sharing

Desired Outcome: Making listening the norm for every session and for each activity within each session. Also, slowing down the "talkers" while encouraging the "non-talkers" by a method that everyone agrees to.

Best Used: Whenever there are small group discussions where the goal is to allow everyone in the group to say at least one thing he or she is thinking or feeling.

"Rules for Simple Sharing" represents a process where small groups can run efficiently yet not fear being dominated by one or two people. These rules require an introduction the first time they are used and work best when they can be given as a handout. It is necessary to remind people about the rules each time they get into groups until the entire group has internalized the rules and can do the process easily and without resistance. The rules are as follows:

1. Each person in the group is asked to share one thought or feeling on the topic at hand. The group will not be successful unless everyone has been given an opportunity to share.

2. When someone shares, other group members can only ask clarifying questions about what was said. An example of a clarifying question is: "Are you saying that . . . ?" or "What did you mean when you said . . . ?" People are asked to refrain from giving their opinions about another person's sharing.

3. Each person is asked to adopt a stance of openness and tolerance for the opinions or statements of others in the group.

4. People are given the option to pass when it is their turn to speak; everyone is encouraged, however, to say something on the topic at hand.

5. Once everyone has been given an opportunity to share, people are asked to go around the circle again, this time commenting on what they heard other people say.

6

Facilitating the Sessions of

Before "I Do"

THE FLOW OF THE SESSIONS

This manual has been prepared keeping in mind that the people who implement the material often make adaptations to the material in their planning and in the actual unfolding of the sessions. The sections in the couple's booklets are designed to be modular in application. This recognizes that program leaders and lead couples often make pastoral decisions to adapt whatever program they are using to meet the needs of their unique setting. The person implementing each session should view the session notes as only one way of implementing the session. There are often various alternatives to implementation on the local level.

Each session has been designed to last between two and three hours. The author will leave it up to the individual to implement a longer or shorter program by combining modules and by picking and choosing from the material present. It is strongly recommended, however, that any adaptation include the section titled "Faith at the Heart of Your Marriage" as well as at least one of the case studies.

It is far easier to implement a couple-to-couple program because the group dynamics are pretty straightforward. Most couples start from the beginning of the material and take a leisurely route from beginning to end. Since there are only two people to plan for, the lead couple has the luxury of more time for each person and need not worry about the complexities of group dynamics.

For those working in a group setting, notes are included under the heading "Group Program." For those who are engaged in a couple-to-couple program, there are implementation notes under the heading "Couple-to-Couple." In planning a group program there is a need to follow a schedule.

Approximate time allowances for implementing each section are given, listed after the heading introducing each section.

For those of you implementing a group program there are more complex group dynamics to consider. Sometimes, you will want to have small group reflection. At other times you will want to have the engaged couples spend time alone with the material. And finally, if you plan on having any "witness talks" by married couples, you will need to factor this into your planning. It goes without saying that there will be more than enough material to occupy a two- to two-and-a-half-hour session, since the more participants there are, the longer it takes to complete exercises and make the transition from one activity to another.

Most of the implementation notes concern specific suggestions for using material. From time to time there are comments listed in italics that cover a more general topic such as covenant or sacrament. The comments are meant for both group and couple-to-couple programs. The most important element of any effective marriage prep program is the witness and participation of the lead couple or team member. The material is meant to facilitate a dialogue and bring the engaged couple to a deeper understanding of their commitment and love for one another. When all is said and done, a newly married couple will remember the people who helped prepare them, not the book they used.

Suggested Outline

SESSION ONE: BUILDING YOUR MARRIAGE ON A SOUND FOUNDATION

Total suggested time: 2 hours, 55 minutes to 3 hours, 5 minutes

Comment: Because of time constraints, you may need to allow less time for some of the sections. Another possibility is to leave a section for the couple to do at home on their own. This will become a necessity if you plan sessions that run for just two hours. For instance, you may choose not to do a section in favor of having a group discussion on one of the case studies. It is recommended that you give enough time for the material on the spirituality of marriage, even if you do not cover all of the material.

1. Welcome and Greeting of Couples (5 min.)

2. Opening Prayer and Overview of Program (10 min.)

Group Program: Use the prayers in the couple's book or have a team member design a prayer service.

Couple-to-Couple: Use one of the prayers in the back of the book, a memorized prayer such as the Our Father, or a spontaneous prayer offered by either member of the lead couple.

3. Sections 1 & 2: Energy, Excitement, & Gifts We Give (15 min.)

Group Program: Have the couples spend time going through each section, answering questions. Then, have each couple pair with another. Each person is to share his or her answer to one item from each section.

Couple-to-Couple: Give the couple time to complete the sections; then ask them to respond to each question one by one or only to the questions that interest them.

4. Sections 3 & 4: Your Expectations & Great Expectations (15 min.)

Group Program: Have the couples do the exercise; then fiancés are to share with each other their responses. The positive expectations that the Church has for an engaged couple's marriage can be stressed in the talk later in the program.

Couple-to-Couple: Have the couple do the exercise on their own expectations. Feel free to raise the issue of the Church's expectation for their happiness and lasting commitment. This might be a good time to stress the covenant relationship that frames the marriage commitment. (See the section "A Sacred Covenant, a Holy Sacrament" on pp. 43–46)

Comment: This is a good time to break the stereotype of the Church as the stern parent ready to reprimand the person who steps out of line. Emphasize with the couple(s) the high hopes and earnest prayer for joy and happiness that the Church has for them. In the group program this can be addressed through the presentation/"witness talk"; in the couple-to-couple program this can be addressed in the normal course of the conversation.

5. Section 5: Realistic Expectations? (30 min.)

Group Program: Have the couples go through these expectations and fill out their responses. Then, divide them into small groups of no more than six people to a group. Ask each person to share a response to at least one question to which he or she responded.

When dividing couples into small groups, you may want to review the Rules for Simple Sharing. Also, the issue of unrealistic expectations can be addressed in a presentation or "witness talk."

A budget sheet is provided in conjunction with this section for couples to do on their own.

Couple-to-Couple: After the couple finishes this section, allow them to go through the expectations at a leisurely pace. Make sure that your personal disclosures from your own marriage facilitate the sharing of the engaged couple. It is appropriate and helpful to talk about how you dealt with your own unrealistic expectations, but be careful to allow the engaged couple to speak, too. If they are eager and excited to share, try to keep them talking.

A budget sheet is provided in conjunction with this section for couples to do on their own.

Comment: Expectations can create ambivalence on the part of a couple getting married. On the one hand, expectations tell us something about the future we want; on the other hand they can become an obligation that we rebel against. As the couple(s) share(s) on this material, be sensitive to any tension surrounding expectations that one or both feel are unattainable or unrealistic. This may be harder to monitor in a group format, but if it does occur, be ready to offer any couple discreet but appropriate counsel. Often, couples need to be reminded that tension over expectations is a normal part of a committed relationship. Look for especially troublesome expectations such as the expectation that marriage will change another's drinking or harmful conflict resolution style (name-calling, hitting, etc.). These call for a different sort of intervention. (See the section "Confidentiality," pp. 60–64)

The desire to change one's spouse is perhaps the biggest stumbling block that trips up a couple early in marriage. It is especially important to address the expectations of each spouse in this area.

Also, be sensitive to how a couple appears to handle conflict. Some of this may begin to surface in the first session. Don't be surprised when you discover that some couples are more open to dealing with anger and conflict. "Anger" and "conflict" are two words that many people don't connect to a healthy marriage. Yet research indicates that as anger and conflict are dealt with and resolved, a marriage is made stronger. It is when anger and conflict are avoided and replayed again and again that real difficulty is created.

6. Speaker/"Witness Talk" (15 min.)

Group Program: This is a good place to have a "witness talk" from someone who has had to adjust his or her expectations in the course of a marriage. This topic can be joined with the notion of "covenant relationship" where there exist both realistic and unrealistic expectations. It is best to make such a talk as experiential as possible while placing stress on how spirituality helped him or her adjust to the reality of being married. It would be ideal if a couple could make this presentation, with each spouse briefly offering his or her own perspective.

7. Break, Group Program Only (10 min. maximum)

8. Sections 6 & 7: Building on Solid Ground & Twelve Foundational Factors (40 min.)

Group Program: This next section is crucial in helping the engaged couple understand that spirituality is holistic, that it includes the entire person. Encourage the couple to see their own religious beliefs and practices as extending into their everyday workweek, their time alone, and their time with friends. Have the couples complete this section in quiet. Then send each engaged couple away to talk privately with each other. Have them report back after thirty minutes.

Couple-to-Couple: Think carefully about how you might present the idea of a spirituality of married life in a positive and interesting way. Where appropriate, speak about your experience concerning what your own faith and spirituality have meant to your marriage. Also, in your own marriage, which foundational factors were fully present at the time of your marriage and which ones did you need to develop through the course of your marriage?

Comment: You may want to facilitate discussion by asking the couple to identify three or four foundational factors that they have either not thought about or that impress them as especially important.

Another approach if time is running short is to have the couple(s) simply check the factors where they think they are doing well, and put a minus sign next to those factors where they wish to improve. You can then encourage the couple(s) to look at the questions sometime in the following week.

9. Case Study (20 min.)

Group Program: Divide the couples into small groups of not more than six people. Assign them one of the case studies and ask them to read it, answer the questions, and then discuss the case.

Couple-to-Couple: Try to leave enough time to discuss at least one of the case studies. Have the couple read through the other case study and answer the related questions during the next week.

Suggested Outline

Session Two: The Two Will Become One

Total suggested time: 1 hour, 40 minutes to 2 hours, 5 minutes

Comment: Because of time constraints, you may need to allow less time for some of the sections. Another possibility is to leave a section for the couple to do at home on their own. This will become a necessity if you plan sessions that run for just two hours. For instance, you may choose not to do a section in favor of having a group discussion on one of the case studies. It is recommended that you give enough time for the material on the spirituality of marriage, even if you do not cover all the material.

1. Opening Prayer (10 min.)

Group Program: Use the prayers in the couple's book or have a team member design a prayer service.

Couple-to-Couple: Use one of the prayers in the back of the book, a memorized prayer such as the Our Father, or a spontaneous prayer offered by either the lead couple or engaged couple.

2. Section 1: Faith at the Heart of Your Marriage (10 min.)

Group Program: Introduce this section by stating that beginning with the second session, the couples will start with a short reflection on the spirituality of marriage. Have the engaged couples take time to read over the section. Then, ask each couple to share their answers with each other for five minutes.

Couple-to-Couple: After checking in with the engaged couple, mention that each session from now on will begin with a short reflection on the spirituality of marriage. Next, ask the couple to read over the section and then answer the questions. Then, have them choose one or two responses to share with you.

3. Section 2: Knowing Yourself (20 min.)

Group Program: Have each person take five minutes to do the exercise. Then, break into small groups of two or three engaged couples. Each person is to share one thing they checked about themselves. Everyone is asked to share at least one thing before anyone shares another item. Let this process continue for fifteen minutes.

Couple-to-Couple: Invite the couple to take five minutes to do the exercise. Then ask them to begin sharing. Some engaged couples want to know as much as possible about the other person and will want to go through the items one at a time. Other couples might want to jump around. Simply ask if either of them wants to begin the sharing; let the couple determine the pace. Intervene by asking questions only if there are long silences.

Comment: Sometimes there is some awkwardness concerning sharing, especially in the beginning of any group. If this appears to be the case you might want to try out the Good and New exercise in the future. (See p. 67.) This exercise gives a simple way to break the ice without taking a lot of time. If you use this exercise in a group format, ask the small groups to begin with it. In a couple-to-couple approach this exercise can be used right after the opening prayer.

4. Sections 3 & 4: Family of Origin's Influence & Factors That Form Relationships (25 min.)

Group Program: Have each person take ten minutes to read through the material and fill out his or her responses to the ten factors. Then, divide into small groups again, asking each person to share one factor that he or she marked "low" and one that he or she marked "high." It is important to remind the groups of the Rules for Simple Sharing, since some people may feel vulnerable in their sharing.

Couple-to-Couple: Have the couple read through the section and make their responses to the exercise. Then work with them through the material. A follow-up question to ask both of them is: "Are there any factors in particular that you want your partner to be aware of as you begin a life together?" You may want to share with the engaged couple where the two of you were with the ten factors when you were first married.

Be sensitive to the fact that this exercise might encourage a deeper storytelling on the part of the engaged couple. It's okay to get "sidetracked" and take longer with the material, especially if it facilitates a deeper sharing between the two.

Comment: One's family of origin can be both a great resource and a great burden. This fact often gives rise to a state of ambivalence in which a person experiences a "love-hate" relationship with his or her family. This is true even for people who come from families that are relatively intact and psychologically healthy. Just separating and becoming independent from one's family of origin can create a powerful emotional reaction. On the one hand a person is excited to be on his or her own, while on the other hand he or she might miss the warmth and protective structure that the family once provided.

All of this becomes more complicated when we consider how many people come from families that are more seriously dysfunctional. Many people, for example, have experienced a family environment that was either overly intrusive or neglectful.

Even when a person experiences these negative influences, however, there is still a tendency to be loyal to one's family. When an engaged couple begins to share their experiences with others, it is important to note that they might minimize any negative influences while idealizing positive ones. This may cause a lead couple or team member to feel that a participant is not being completely honest, but it's important to remember that people tend to share more deeply as they begin to trust more. If you encounter any resistance in this exercise, remind yourself that as the couple begins to develop a deeper trust and rapport, their sharing will most likely deepen.

5. Break, Group Program Only (10 min.)

6. Section 5: Blending Your Approaches (10 min.)

Group Program: This section will be done in two parts. The first part is to be done before the witness talk; the second part involves a discussion of the material after the witness talk. Allow the participants time to read the material and then go through the exercises. Tell them that this is preparation for the talk, which will recount one couple's experience of how they blended the various aspects of personal habits, friends, work, and social interests.

Couple-to-Couple: It will be helpful to share your own experience of having blended personal habits, friends, work, and social interests into your early married life. Give the couple time to go through the material and complete the exercises. Then, move through the material at a leisurely pace, sharing your own experiences when appropriate. Remember, your personal disclosure is meant to facilitate a deepening of sharing and trust. Be careful not to dominate or talk too long when you share. Personal disclosure is especially helpful when the engaged couple comes to an issue where there is obvious tension or where they feel stuck. Your sharing can help to reassure them that difficulties can be worked through.

7. Witness Talk, Group Program Only (15 min.)

Group Program: The witness talk, if included, can address one couple's experience of blending the various interests outlined above. This talk can be delivered by a couple or by one spouse. Again, it's best if the speaker(s) can make realistic connections to a spirituality of marriage as it relates to this topic.

After the witness talk is finished, put the couples into small groups of two to three couples. Ask participants to share one or two items from the exercises in section 5; they can also address issues and themes from the witness talk they just heard. Keep in mind the Rules for Simple Sharing. You may have to remind the couples about the importance of having everyone share at least once.

8. Sections 6 & 7: Marriage as Journey & Constructing Your Timeline (30 min.)

Group Program: Have the engaged couples read over silently the material in this section and construct their timelines. Then, have the engaged couples spend time alone sharing the results of their individual timelines. After a suitable time bring them back together. Ask for a few volunteers from the larger group to respond to the following questions:

Did you learn anything new about yourself as a result of doing the timeline?

Did you learn anything new about your fiancé as a result of this exercise?

Couple-to-Couple: Allow time for the couple to read through the material and complete the timeline. Then, have them share their results in a leisurely fashion. Ask the same questions given in the paragraph above.

Comment: This may be a good time to ask the couple(s) to reread the introduction to the couple's workbook since it has an imaginative journey based on the gospel passage, "The Road to Emmaus" (Lk 24:13–35).

9. Case Study (20 min.)

Group Program: Divide the couples into small groups of two to three couples. Assign a case to each group. Allow a few minutes for individuals to read the case and respond to the discussion questions. Have the small groups focus on their answers to the questions following each case.

Couple-to-Couple: Ask the couple to select a case, read it over, and respond to the reflection questions. Then, facilitate a discussion of the case.

Suggested Outline

SESSION THREE: ESTABLISHING EMOTIONAL AND SEXUAL INTIMACY

Total suggested time: 2 hours, 30 minutes to 3 hours

1. Opening Prayer (10 min.)

Group Program: Use the prayers in the couple's book or have a team member design a prayer service.

Couple-to-Couple: Use one of the prayers in the back of the book, a memorized prayer such as the Our Father, or a spontaneous prayer offered by either the lead couple or engaged couple.

2. Section 1: Faith at the Heart of Your Marriage (10 min.)

Group Program: Ask everyone to read over this section and respond to the reflection questions that follow. Then, for five minutes, have each engaged couple process how each person responded.

Couple-to-Couple: Give the couple time to read over the material and answer the reflection questions. Then allow for processing of each person's responses.

Comment: The notion of a sacrament as an efficacious sign that points to a deeper reality rooted in Christ may be familiar to someone raised in a Catholic family. But to others it may be totally new. Keep in mind, too, that many couples share an interreligious experience. One person in the pair may be Protestant, Jewish, or Muslim or may profess no belief whatsoever. It may be a good idea to be ready at least to pursue the notion of sacramentality a bit more deeply if the couple indicates interest. For reference, see chapter 3, "Understanding the Sacrament of Marriage."

3. Sections 2 & 3: Emotional Nurturing and Intimacy & What Is Intimacy? (25 min.)

Group Program: Have the participants spend time reading over the material in section 2 and answer the questions that follow. Then, have them go on and complete the exercises in section 3. After everyone has completed these two sections, divide the couples into small groups of no more than three couples. Invite each person to share at least one response from section 2. Then, after everyone has shared at least one of his or her responses, have the groups go on to share responses from section 3. After the groups have concluded, in the large group, ask for two to three responses from the engaged couples on the following questions:

Did any of you learn anything new concerning how your fiancé defines intimacy?

Did you learn anything new concerning what is easy for your fiancé to offer you when you're hassled or upset? What is difficult?

Couple-to-Couple: Have the couple take time to read over sections 2 and 3. Then, ask them to respond to the reflection questions following section 2. Be ready to follow up when an individual states that he or she has changed as a result of falling in love with his or her fiancé. Most of these changes will be for the better. It will be a rare occurrence when a person states that knowing his fiancé has made him or her worse off. If this occurs this may be a sign of trouble, and you need to be ready to pursue this. (Refer to the section "Confidentiality," pp. 60–64, for help in this regard.)

After participants have shared their responses to section 2, ask them to respond to section 3. Be ready to ask follow-up questions. See the questions given above for the group program.

4. Section 4: What's Love Got to Do With It? (20 min.)

Group Program: Introduce this section by stating that the couples will be asked to look at three different components of married love. Have them take time to read the material and then respond to the two questions that follow. Then, break the large group into small groups of not more than three couples and ask the participants to share their responses.

Couple-to-Couple: Have the couple take time to read through the material in this section, then to answer the questions that follow. Feel free to share with the couple how your percentages have changed throughout the history of your relationship. For instance, you may have had a great deal of "love as feeling" early on in your relationship, only to redefine this when your children began to arrive and you had less time to spend on the feeling aspects of your relationship.

Comment: This section makes some important distinctions concerning what we mean by married love. There is, of course, a popular notion of love as a passionate, intense feeling for the other, popularized in the music of the Top 40. The only problem with this notion is that it cannot sustain a marriage when the feeling begins to fade. Married couples who have been together several years realize that their needs to be something more than just feeling. This is where love as a committed stance and process of intimacy comes into play. It is important to stress with the engaged couple the necessity of these other two forms of love. It is hoped that the engaged couple will see that love is not just a given in their relationship but that it is also something that can be worked at and created again and again.

5. Break, Group Program Only (10 min.)

6. Witness Talk, Group Program Only (15 min.)

Group Program: The witness talk, if included, can be one person's (or one couple's) experience about how intimacy was and is created in the marital relationship. It can draw material from the previous sections about how often men and women take the expectations of the other for granted. We think we know how to meet the needs of our spouses without really checking out our assumptions with our spouse. A talk such as this might also focus on the third aspect of married love, that of love as a process of growth, reconciliation, and forgiveness that creates a lifetime of intimacy. A couple (or individual) can address how their notion of love changed to include a continual process of communication, forgiveness, etc. Finally, time can be given to highlighting the National Conference of Catholic Bishops' criteria for developing a mature conscience in the area of sex and sexuality.

7. Section 5: Rules for Intimacy (15 min.)

Group Program: This section follows easily after a witness talk, especially if the talk addresses the creation of intimacy within a marriage. Have the couples read through this section and respond to the "intimacy rules" listed, checking the appropriate responses. Then, break into small groups of not more than three couples. Have each person in the group share at least one thing that is easy for him or her to do and one thing that is difficult to do from the exercise; have the group share any other "rule" that they have listed at the end of the exercise.

Couple-to-Couple: Have the couple fill out their responses to this section. Then, ask them to go through the material together, giving their responses to what is difficult and what is easy for each of them to do regarding intimacy.

Comment: This might be a good time to gently suggest that all of us from time to time need to turn to an outside source, like a priest or therapist, for help when our relationship begins to bog down. Intimacy is easier to sustain in the beginning of a relationship, and it can be sustained and deepened throughout the relationship if a couple takes the time and energy to foster it. Keep in mind that 50 percent of the marriages that fail in the United States fail within the first seven years. This tells us that many couples do not weather the first, early crisis of intimacy and communication.

8. Sections 6 & 7: Exploring Sexual Love & Taking Responsibility for Married Love (15 min.)

Group Program: Have the couples read through the material from these two sections and complete the exercises. Then, split the individual engaged couples up so that partners can discuss their answers to the exercises privately. Explain to them that it is important that they have a common understanding of and clear expectations for sexual intimacy. Ask them to pay close attention to any areas where there are clear disagreements. When they come back together again as a large group, if there is time, this may be a good time to clarify any questions regarding Church teaching on this subject.

Couple-to-Couple: Have the couple go through the two sections and respond to the exercise. Tell them that if there is any area that they do not wish to discuss with you, that you will respect their wishes. Stress with them the importance of a common understanding of and clear expectations for sexual intimacy. Your role as a lead couple is to serve as a facilitator and resource to them. It is hoped that by the third session enough trust is developed between you and the engaged couple that they can share freely their responses.

Comment: The section "Exploring Sexual Love" contains the National Conference of Catholic Bishops' criteria for the development of a mature conscience in the area of sex and sexuality within marriage. It is a good idea to point out these criteria to the couple(s) so that they realize that the Church's teaching on sex and sexuality is based on an articulated theology of the human person. Another reason for noting these criteria is that many couples may be surprised that they actually agree with the criteria, and that they have had misconceptions of the Church's teaching based on media accounts, which often portray an overly simplistic notion.

9. Section 8: Christian Marriage and the Integration of Erotic and Agape Love (20 min.)

Group Program: Allow each person to read the material for this section and to answer questions 1 and 2 on his or her own. Then, break into small groups of two or three couples. Have each person share one hopeful thing he or she sees in today's cultural portrayal of love and sexuality. If time allows, ask the partners to sit together to respond to question 3.

Couple-to-Couple: Allow time for the couple to read the material and respond to the reflection questions individually. Then ask them to share their responses to the reflection questions.

10. Section 9: Marriage as a Conversation (20 min.)

Group Program: Allow time to read through this section and for each person to give his or her response to the exercises and questions. Then, break into small groups of not more than three couples. Have each person share one thing he or she is doing well with, one thing he or she wants to improve on, and one response to the reflection questions at the end of this section.

Couple-to-Couple: Allow time to read through this section and invite the couple to do the exercises that follow. Then, ask them to name one or two items where each is doing well and one or two items where each wants to improve. Have them also give their responses to the reflection questions.

11. Case Study (20 min.)

Group Program: Break the large group into small groups of not more than three couples. Assign each group a case study and allow enough time to read through the case study and answer the questions. Then, ask each person in the group to share at least one answer to the reflection questions. Make sure that the groups remember the Rules for Simple Sharing, and that everyone feels that he or she can share at least one response. Remember, cases can be given as "homework" if you don't have enough time to get to them.

Couple-to-Couple: Ask the couple to choose one of the case studies, read through it, and answer the questions. Then, ask them to share their responses. If you have enough time, go on to the next case. Remember, case studies can be given as "homework" if you don't have enough time to get to them.

Suggested Outline

SESSION FOUR: A NEW FAMILY CIRCLE

Total suggested time: 2 hours, 15 minutes to 2 hours, 40 minutes

1. Opening Prayer (10 min.)

Group Program: Use the prayers in the couple's book or have a team member design a prayer service.

Couple-to-Couple: Use one of the prayers in the couple's book, a memorized prayer such as the Our Father, or a spontaneous prayer offered by either the lead couple or engaged couple.

2. Section 1: Faith at the Heart of Your Marriage (10 min.)

Group Program: Have the couples take time to read the short section and give their responses to the questions. Have each engaged couple pair up with another engaged couple to go through their responses. By now the couples should have developed enough trust to share on the level of faith and spirituality.

Couple-to-Couple: Have the couple take time to read the short section and give their responses to the questions. Then, take them through their responses. Be ready to have them react to the quote "You can fire an employee, but you can't fire a family member."

3. Sections 2 & 3: How Were You Parented? & Your Family Position (15 min.)

Group Program: Introduce this exercise by stating that it is time to get in touch with how our families have influenced our formation. Have them fill out the exercise and then break into small groups of no more than three couples. Remind them of the Rules for Simple Sharing and have each of them share the characteristics that he or she selected along with the responses to the two reflection questions. This is also a good place to have couples share one or two photos from their own family of origin. See "Sharing of Personal Symbols," page 68.

Couple-to-Couple: Have the couple complete the exercise and the two reflection questions. Then, invite each person to share the characteristics he or she selected along with the responses to the questions. This is also a good place to have couples share one or two photos from their own family of origin. See "Sharing of Personal Symbols" on page 68.

Comment: The way we are raised exercises subtle yet real influences on us. Not only our parents but also our siblings give us behavioral criteria for our selection of a mate. For instance, a male raised in a family where all his siblings were male might have a more difficult time later on in life understanding the needs of his wife, especially if his relationship with his mother was distant or conflictual. Another married man, later in the marriage, might realize that he didn't "marry his mother" as much as he "married his sister."

4. *Section 4: Parenting Styles in Your Family of Origin (15 min.)*

Group Program: Have the couples take time to complete the two exercises on parenting styles. Then, have them pair up with another couple to share their responses. Tell them to be sure to cover the reflection questions at the end of the section, since it is possible that many of the participants experienced a blend of two of the three styles of parenting.

Couple-to-Couple: Allow time for the couple to go through the exercises in this section and to consider the follow-up questions. Have them share their answers. Place emphasis on the fact that their responses represent their experience, and that there are no "right" or "wrong" answers.

Comment: Our experience of our family of origin can bring up a great deal of ambivalence. On the one hand we tend to be loyal to our families; on the other hand we may also have some unresolved issues with our parents that bring up feelings of frustration and anger. Be ready to reassure the participants that these exercises are not about assigning blame or expressing anger, although that may occur. Rather, the purpose of these exercises is to allow the participants to reach a level of awareness that may move them to resolve any unfinished business, thus allowing them more freedom in their future relationship with their spouse.

5. Section 5: Your Parents' Disciplinary Techniques (20 min.)

Group Program: Ask the couples to read through the material and respond to the exercise. Then, divide the couples into groups no larger than three couples. Have them share their responses to the exercise and the following reflection questions. Ask them to be aware of the Rules for Simple Sharing and put stress on sharing the reflection questions, as these questions point them toward their future as parents. Stress with all the couples the importance of honoring someone's decision to pass and not share, since this material can evoke powerful memories that some people do not want to process in this type of setting.

Couple-to-Couple: Ask the couple to read through the material and respond to the exercise. Be aware of the fact that this material can evoke deep emotions, especially if a person has experienced a negative form of discipline such as shame. Preface the sharing by stating that if there is any material that each person does not want to share, this will be respected.

Comment: It may be a good idea to have ready a few names of therapists and family counselors that can help someone sort through the power of his or her family of origin. If you notice someone upset or especially quiet, this may be an indication that the material has struck a deeper, more conflictual chord with that person. The sessions themselves are not an appropriate vehicle for therapy, but a lead couple or group leader can go a long way in encouraging a person to resolve issues that are unfinished.

6. Break, Group Program Only (10 min.)

7. Witness Talk, Group Program Only (15 min.)

Group Program: It's recommended that a witness talk done by either one person or a married couple serve as a bridge between the material in the first half of this session and the last half. A talk should cover the speaker's experience of having been formed by his or her family and how that formation affected the early years of marriage. Then, the talk can lead into how his or her family of origin experience shaped the early years of child rearing, including pregnancy, childbirth, and the transition period that followed.

8. Section 6: Becoming a Parent (15 min.)

Group Program: Allow time for everyone to fill out this exercise. Then, ask each couple to pair off with another couple. Ask them to share their responses to the checklist and their responses to the hopes and fears they have as they imagine bringing children into the world.

Couple-to-Couple: Allow time for the couple to fill out the exercise. Then, ask them to share their responses. This may be a good time for you to share some of your own experiences. When the couple describes something that scares them, for instance, you can reassure them by admitting that the same thing was scary for you (assuming it was, of course). Pay particular attention to the hopes and fears that they have as they imagine bringing children into the world.

9. Section 7: Marriage as Growing a Garden (30 min.)

Group Program: Have the couples read through the material and respond to the reflection questions. Then, have each of the engaged couples spend time by themselves processing the material. After allowing about fifteen minutes for processing the reflection questions, bring the couples back to the large group to discuss their responses with everyone. Pay particular attention to the group's response to the notion of Baptism. Stress that the Church wants to be an active part of their lives not only when they marry but when they have children as well.

Couple-to-Couple: Allow time for the couple to read through the material and respond to the reflection questions. Then, ask them to share their responses to the questions.

Comment: Don't be afraid of silences. Sometimes couples might find it difficult to share on the topic of spirituality. This is because we generally are not used to talking about our faith and spirituality on a daily basis. Thus, a couple might fall silent when faced with more serious questions about their spirituality. Be comfortable with silence. Remember, just about everyone feels awkward when there is silence. If you can keep silent longer, chances are an engaged person will break the silence and begin sharing. Then, you're off and running!

10. Case Study (20 min.)

Group Program: Break couples into small groups of not more than three couples. Assign each group a case study and ask them to spend five minutes reading over the case and answering the questions. Then, ask each person to share his or her response to at least one of the questions.

Couple-to-Couple: Have the couple select which case they want to discuss and then read through it silently. After they have read the case, have them write their answers to the reflection questions. Then allow for discussion.

Suggested Outline

SESSION FIVE: DEALING WITH CONFLICT

Total suggested time: 2 hours, 5 minutes to 2 hours, 40 minutes

1. Opening Prayer (10 min.)

Group Program: Use the prayers in the couple's book or have a team member design a prayer service.

Couple-to-Couple: Use one of the prayers in the couple's book, a memorized prayer such as the Our Father, or a spontaneous prayer offered by either the lead couple or engaged couple.

2. Section 1: Faith at the Heart of Your Marriage (10 min.)

Group Program: Have the couples read through the material and give their responses to the reflection questions. Then, have each couple pair up with another couple and discuss their responses to this section.

Couple-to-Couple: Invite the couple to read through the material and give their responses to the reflection that follows. Don't forget to give your own reaction to the material.

3. Section 2: Getting in Touch With Your Conflict Style (20 min.)

Group Program: Explain to the couples that this session will cover not only the way we think and respond to conflict but also practicing new ways of resolving conflict. Ask the couples to read through the section and then do the exercise that follows. Then, break the couples into small groups of not more than three couples. Have them share their responses to the checklist as well as the reflection questions.

Couple-to-Couple: After explaining the purpose of the session (see above) have the couple take time to read the material in the section and complete the exercise and questions that follow. Then, take them through the material, being sensitive to the questions on family of origin.

4. Section 3: Conflict Resolution Begins With Clear Communication (25 min.)

Group Program: This next session introduces material concerning how we communicate with each other. Invite the couples to read through the section. When they are finished, summarize the material on pages 91–93, emphasizing the importance of what is actually spoken versus what is communicated by tone of voice and body posture. Then, invite the couples to answer the reflection questions. After they have done that, ask each engaged couple to discuss with each other their responses to these questions.

Couple-to-Couple: Have the couple read through the material in this section. Then, have them answer the first reflection question. Begin by asking them if they find anything surprising in this material (pp. 91–93). Also, ask them if the pattern of "feel, think, do" makes sense to them. Be prepared to give an example from your own experience. Then, go on to the final question about the block to listening. Ask each person to give his or her response to this question.

Comment: Listening is an art form that is taken for granted. The tendency is for us to read the other person's mind and assume that we know what he or she is going to say in advance. In marriages that have failed, respondents indicated that poor communication and conflict resolution skills ranked high on the list of factors that led to the marital breakdown. It makes sense to practice some skill building, but the trouble is that when communication is practiced, it often becomes artificial and feels forced. You may receive some resistance from participants over this; if so, use the above information as a way of persuading the participants that it is in their own best interest to take a look at more effective communication and conflict resolution skills.

5. Sections 4 & 5: Requests of the Other & Good Communication Takes Practice (20 min.)

Group Program: Introduce these sections by stating that section 4 gives a model for communicating clearly and directly with another person. Give the participants time to read over these two sections. Then, have them focus on a positive event that happened in the past week and complete the exercise in section 5. After they have done this, pair the couples up. Have one couple act as an "observer couple" and the other as the "communicating couple." Each person is asked to communicate the positive event to his or her fiancé; after both members of the couple has done this, they are to receive feedback from the "observer couple" whether they were clear in describing the event, their feeling reactions, the consequences, their thoughts, and what they want in the future.

Couple-to-Couple: Allow the couple time to read through the material and complete the exercise in section 5. Then, act as the "observer couple" and invite each person to share his or her communication of the positive event that occurred this past week. Give the couple feedback on how clearly they described the event, their feeling reactions, the consequences, their thoughts, and what they want in the future. Be ready to use examples from your own marriage to make clear the benefit of direct communication.

6. Break, Group Program Only (10 min.)

7. Witness Talk, Group Program Only (15 min.)

Group Program: This is a good time to consider having a "group within a group." See page 69 of this manual for details. Place six chairs in the middle of the room and arrange all the other chairs around the outside so that there is a large outer circle and a smaller inner circle. Invite four married people to take the circle on the inside. Ask them to begin to talk about times in their lives when they resolved conflict successfully, and what obstacles must be overcome in resolving conflict. Before the exercise begins, tell those on the outer circle that whenever they have a question or comment, they can come into the inner circle and take one of the empty chairs. After they have asked their question and received an answer, or after they have made their comment, they can return to the outer circle.

Another variation to this exercise is to have a small group of women take the inner circle and then discuss some of the more difficult aspects to resolving conflict. Then, a small group of men are asked to take the inner circle and discuss the same question.

After the discussion goes on for ten or fifteen minutes, ask everyone to move to the outer circle. Ask those who were quiet for their reactions and observations regarding the exercise. Ask if anyone learned anything new about conflict and conflict resolution.

8. Sections 6 & 7: Knowing How to Fight Fairly & Conflict Checklist (15 min.)

Group Program: The list entitled "Conflict Rules" has a step-by-step process that couples can follow when faced with conflict. There are two choices that can be made concerning the couples practicing these steps: they can practice during the program, or you can assign this as something to work on during the week. In any case, invite them to read the rules and then follow the directions underneath the rules.

Next, give the couples time to go through the conflict checklist (section 7). Then, break them into small groups of not more than three couples. Have each person share his or her response to at least one item.

Couple-to-Couple: Make a decision as to whether you will have the couple process the "conflict rules" during the session or later during the week. If you defer to later during the week, make sure that the couple understand how to complete the exercise. Next, ask them to go through the conflict checklist, giving their responses to the statements. Then, have them share all of their responses or the ones that strike them the most.

Comment: There are some particularly harmful ways of communicating that can worsen conflict and inflict fatal harm on a relationship. According to John Gottman, constant criticism, "stonewalling," contempt, and constant defensiveness are four serious, harmful factors that can destroy a relationship.[27] Also, explosive rage and/or violence should be taken as a warning sign. If anyone gives an indication that any of these factors exist in his or her relationship, it might be a good idea to consider making a referral for counseling. Sometimes people will make joking reference to negative ways of communicating and conflict resolution; this could be an indication of a more serious underlying issue. On the other hand, many people bring into marriage a mixture of healthy and unhealthy ways of relating.

9. Section 8: Marriage as Friendship (20 min.)

Group Program: Have the couples read through the material and respond to the exercise and question. Then, have each engaged couple spend time alone sharing their responses with each other.

Couple-to-Couple: Have the couple read through the material, respond to the exercise, and write the letter to their partner. Then, have them talk about the responses they listed. Be ready to share your experience concerning how you grew together as friends.

10. Case Study (15 min.)

Group Program: Break couples into small groups of not more than three couples. Assign each group a case study and ask them to spend five minutes reading over the case and answering the questions. Then, ask each person to share his or her response to at least one of the questions.

Couple-to-Couple: Have the couple select which case they want to discuss and then read through it silently. After they have read the case, have them write their answers to the reflection questions. Then allow for discussion.

Suggested Outline

SESSION SIX: FACING CHANGE AND KEEPING YOUR FOUNDATION INTACT

Total suggested time: 2 hours, 15 minutes to 2 hours, 40 minutes

1. Opening Prayer (10 min.)

Group Program: Use the prayers in the couple's book or have a team member design a prayer service.

Couple-to-Couple: Use one of the prayers in the couple's book, a memorized prayer such as the Our Father, or a spontaneous prayer offered by either the lead couple or engaged couple.

2. Section 1: Faith at the Heart of Your Marriage (10 min.)

Group Program: Invite the couples to read over the section and then respond to the reflection questions that follow. Then, ask the individual engaged couples to spend time giving their responses to the reflection questions.

Couple-to-Couple: Invite the couple to read over the section and respond to the reflection questions. Then have them share their responses. Be ready to share how the two of you have balanced individual and couple volunteer work.

3. Section 2: Change Happens (20 min.)

Group Program: Have the couples complete the exercise on change. Then, have each engaged couple pair with another and share how they responded to the exercise.

Couple-to-Couple: Have the couple complete the exercise on change. Then, invite them to share with you their responses to the exercise.

4. Section 3: Something Lost . . . Something Gained (20 min.)

Group Program: Introduce this section by stating that important changes often require us to face leaving something behind while gaining something important. Read through the first two examples of "loss and gain," and then invite the couples to read through the rest of the material. Invite the couples to complete the exercise described in the text. Next, divide couples into small groups of no more than three couples per group. Ask each person to share one change with his or her small group (two if there is time). Make sure that participants know they have a right to pass if they feel the change listed is too personal to share.

Couple-to-Couple: Take time in going over the first two examples of change in this section with the couple. Then, invite them to read this section and reflect on the exercise that is described in the text. When they are ready, ask each of them to share his or her responses with you. Be ready to share significant changes from your married life.

5. Section 4: Are You Stressed Out? (15 min.)

Group Program: Ask the couples to complete this next section on stress. Where the checklist provides a space for "other," have them consider wedding planning as a stressor. After they complete the exercise, allow time for individual couples to process the results together.

Couple-to-Couple: Ask the couple to complete this next section keeping in mind the above suggestion that wedding planning can be a significant stressor. After the couple has completed the exercise, have them share their responses. Also, be ready to share with the couple the times in your own marriage when the two of you had to deal with the impact of stress. Make sure, however, that you do not dominate and take away from the couple's own processing of the stress that they currently experience.

Comment: Relationships often are the first victims of a life lived under high stress. The symptoms of burnout and depression are surprisingly similar: loss of concentration, sleep disturbances, over- or under-eating, irritability, fits of anger, feelings of desperation. Many marriages are negatively affected just by the fast pace of life, workplace anxiety, and the like. Even a "simple" thing like wedding planning can cause such stress in us; it is a known fact that engaged couples often experience increased tension and arguing as the wedding day approaches.

Your role as a lead couple or team member may be simply validating that an engaged couple's stress is on the rise and helping them understand that this is a very normal occurrence. Sometimes an engaged couple will disclose that they (or at least one of them) are under an extraordinary amount of stress. For instance, an engaged person might have a close friend or relative with a serious illness, or be dealing with a serious job issue at the same time he or she is preparing for the wedding. In this case, be ready to provide a sympathetic ear. Often just naming his or her stress is enough to allow a person to feel more in control of fast-paced days.

There are, of course, healthy and unhealthy ways to deal with stress. If a couple shares that there is an increase in alcohol consumption, it may be important to pursue this and ask for more clarification. Certainly, there is a difference between a sustained pattern of alcohol abuse and drinking as a reaction to increased stress. The feelings of the person who has noticed this behavior are crucial. It is important to emphasize that drinking to relieve stress can be harmful to the relationship without implying that the behavior is necessarily "alcoholic." It may be important to suggest getting an assessment from a qualified alcoholism counselor if the behavior is clearly an issue. See the section "Confidentiality" for a more thorough discussion on drinking.

6. Break, Group Program Only (10 min.)

7. Witness Talk, Group Program Only (15 min.)

Group Program: This is a good time to have someone address the aspect of change throughout the course of a relationship. A speaker can address the issue of how one changes and develops personally, and the impact that this can have on one's relationship with one's spouse. There are other changes to consider as well—for example, the effect of job loss, relocation, health difficulties etc. on the relationship. Make sure that you do not make this presentation a "litany of bad things" that can happen in a relationship. Rather, model hope and resiliency to the couples so that they understand that change does not necessarily have to have negative consequences.

8. Sections 5 & 6: Caring for Yourself and Your Relationship & Developing Rituals of Intimacy and Re-Creation (25 min.)

Group Program: Allow time for the couples to complete the exercises in these two sections. Then invite each couple to pair up with another engaged couple. Ask them to share at least one thing that they do to care for themselves and one unhealthy way they care for themselves when they are under stress. Then, ask them to share with each other the rituals of intimacy and caring that they have identified in the final section.

Couple-to-Couple: Allow time for the couple to complete the exercises in the next two sections. Then, invite the couple to share their responses to how they care for themselves both positively and negatively. Also invite them to share with each other how they want to create rituals of intimacy and care. Don't forget to share with the couple what each of you do to take care of yourselves and what you do together to enhance and deepen your relationship.

9. Section 7: Holiness Is Wholeness (20 min.)

Group Program: Invite the participants to read through the section and then answer the reflection questions that follow. Then, divide the couples into small groups of not more than three couples per group. Ask each person to share his or her responses to the questions. Remind groups of the Rules for Simple Sharing and suggest that they might want to take the questions in sequence so that each person has a chance to say at least one thing.

Couple-to-Couple: Allow time for the couple to read through the section and answer the reflection questions that follow. Then, invite them to share their responses to the questions. Be ready to pick up on the questions involving suffering since it is more than likely that each person will know someone who has suffered a great deal for no apparent reason. Also, when they mention the couple that they admire, be ready to probe as to what it is about that couple that makes them a model of resiliency.

Comment: The question of suffering is perhaps the hardest and oldest question asked of religious systems. It challenges our expectations and assumptions about what life is all about. Many of us have positive expectations of the future and are not prepared for the bad things that can come so suddenly.

This raises the larger question of what it means to be holy in today's world with its many demands and unseen dangers. Even if we don't suffer major tragedy, we are pulled in many diverse directions by the demands of our jobs, children, and other relationships. Given this reality, Jesus' call to not worry about our future can seem to be idealistic and naive. Yet it also can seem to be grounded in a very deep wisdom: that ultimately it is God who is in charge of the universe.

10. Case Study (15 min.)

Group Program: Break couples into small groups of not more than three couples. Assign each group a case study and ask them to spend five minutes reading over the case and answering the questions. Then, ask each person to share his or her response to at least one of the questions.

Couple-to-Couple: Have the couple select which case they want to discuss. After they have read the case, have them write their answers to the reflection questions. Then allow for discussion.

7

Preparing for Second Marriage or
Convalidation Using

Catholic Remarriage: A Workbook for Couples

As a priest, deacon, or LEM working in marriage preparation ministry, you know the complexity of the task at hand when you assist couples in which one or both partners have been previously married. Working with people who have endured the heartache of divorce or the death of a spouse demands great pastoral sensitivity. Like all couples preparing for marriage, these men and women deserve the best pastoral care that the Church has to offer as they prepare for remarriage or convalidation.

In its most common form, convalidation is when a civilly married couple renews their consent (marriage vows) in the presence of the Church's minister, thereby entering into a valid Christian (or sacramental) marriage. Sometimes this is a very simple and private event. Other times, a couple chooses a more public celebration. Occasionally a marriage is validated by sanation. This is done by the action of a bishop or the Holy See, or the proper delegate of either. Because sanation does not require the renewal of consent by either party, you will not likely be working with couples utilizing this process.

As you know, anyone who is preparing for a second marriage or convalidation in the Roman Catholic Church must receive a declaration of nullity for the previous marriage from a diocesan tribunal before the second marriage or the convalidation can take place. This declaration of nullity is simply a statement acknowledging that the first marriage was somehow flawed at its inception. What appeared to be a valid Christian marriage, in fact, was not. Increasingly, annulment comes with a requirement that the person receiving it must participate in some form of pastoral counseling prior to contracting a second marriage or convalidation in the Church.

The couples you work with in these situations present a wide range of circumstances and needs. Many are already living together, some for many years. Other couples are already well into a second civil marriage and now seek convalidation in the Church. Still other couples will have one partner preparing for a second marriage while the other partner prepares for his or her first marriage. Similarly, many couples seek convalidation of an already well-established civil marriage that is a first for one partner while a second for the other. Yet other couples have one partner who has been divorced and the other widowed. Assisting all these couples, with their wide array of circumstances and needs is complicated at best. At worst, it is dizzying and exhausting. This section on using *Catholic Remarriage: A Workbook for Couples* is meant to help you.

USING THIS RESOURCE

Catholic Remarriage is a resource for pastoral counseling and so differs significantly from other marriage preparation resources. It is meant to assist you in your work, enhancing your effort, not comprising the whole of it. The first five chapters of this *Combined Leader's Guide* provide many useful ideas about how to work with a couple, dealing with resistance, and other issues of being a good facilitator. The chapters suggest how to greet the couple, what to expect, and how to keep sessions flowing. I urge you to consult these early chapters as you work with the following material.

Catholic Remarriage can be used by you as an individual pastoral minister or in a well-developed and well-supervised couple-to-couple program. While the workbook is written with individual couples in mind, you may find it beneficial to adapt some of the chapters and exercises for use in small groups of two or more couples with similar circumstances. **Use the book in a flexible manner, picking and choosing which sections to use with each couple or small group and in which order.** Consider it raw material that you can custom fit according to the particular needs of individual couples. Most of the exercises should be completed by each partner individually and then discussed together with you.

The offerings of this book flow from assessing the relationship, to identifying problem areas, to addressing specific problems couples might be facing. Not all couples will benefit from each chapter, nor from every exercise within any given chapter. Again, it will fall largely to you to determine how much of the material to use and when to use it. For instance, a couple that has been married for thirteen years and exhibits excellent communication skills will have very different needs than a couple preparing to begin what will be a second marriage for both of the partners. A couple for whom the coming marriage is a first for one partner and a second for the other may need yet a different set of materials or at least different emphases. Many couples will benefit from working through all the chapters, no matter what their situation. The chapters are arranged as follows:

1. Christian Marriage: Our Context and Our Goal

The opening chapter sets the stage for all the work of this book. Because the goal here is for a couple to enter and be successful at Christian marriage, it is important to talk about just what that means. The chapter addresses marriage as a sacramental covenant and helps the couple to explore together, with you, just how they can appropriate that meaning in their relationship.

2. Assessing Your Relationship

This chapter allows a couple to look at what went wrong in a previous marriage and identify any areas where closure still needs to be worked out. At the same time, the chapter assesses the strengths and weaknesses of a couple concerning communication and conflict resolution. At the end of the chapter, both you and the couple should have a good idea of what areas require additional attention.

3. Creating Relationship Resiliency

This chapter looks at the present relationship of the couple and takes each partner through a process of understanding how solid, healthy relationships are built and sustained. At the same time, the couple will be able to understand if there are any outstanding challenges facing them concerning how resilient their present relationship is.

4. Communicating and Negotiating Effectively

This chapter takes the couple through a process of understanding how to communicate better, especially when there is tension. It helps them to develop skills for negotiating fairly in order to get their individual and shared needs met.

5. Dealing With Conflict

This chapter will explore with the couple how each partner approaches conflict. It also looks at the gifts, challenges, and pitfalls of their approach, and how they might be able to manage conflict more successfully.

6. Parenting in Blended Families

This chapter will allow couples who have children to explore the challenges and promises of a blended family as well as the skills and efforts needed in parenting with former spouses.

7. Cultivating a Forgiving Spirit

This is a chapter on spirituality, and one that may be greatly needed by your couple. Having endured the breakup of a marriage, one or both of the partners may quite possibly experience a difficult time with trust and forgiveness. This chapter can assist in the process of letting go and moving on.

8. Growing Into a Mature Spirituality

This chapter emphasizes how important spirituality is in maintaining a mature relationship. It asks the couple to consider some themes that link them with the wider Church.

Each session concludes with a case illustration and a section on spirituality. The case illustrations are presented with the hope that the couple will be able to further explore any unresolved issues that face them by looking at another couple's situation. A mature spirituality is a very important characteristic to any successful marriage, and it is important that the couple takes responsibility for it together.

OF SPECIAL CONCERN

The Situation of Those Civilly Married for Some Years Who Have Now Secured an Annulment

When working with those who have been civilly married before, you will often find that the couple is well adjusted and reports no serious problem in their relationship. Also, the couple might question the length of the preparation since they already have been married for some years. It is best to acknowledge this if it is the case and to invite the couple to help construct the agenda with you. For instance, if they both admit that improving their communication with each other is a goal, then the material on communication and possible conflict resolution might be the most important. Also, if you use any marriage inventories in your preparation, this will help identify more specific areas of preparation.

First Marriage / Second Marriage

Most of the material presented here is written for those who have experienced divorce. But many times there will be one person who has never been married before preparing to marry someone who has been married and divorced. Such a couple needs special attention when using this material. While much of the work will fall to the previously married partner, it is crucial that the two work together as much as possible.

The person for whom this is a first marriage may sometimes feel at a disadvantage because he or she doesn't know firsthand the experience of being married. He or she also can never fully appreciate how the other partner was wounded by the events that led to the failure of the first marriage. He or she may not fully grasp the fear or uncertainty that the other partner brings. At the same time, the partner who has lived through divorce will likely have fears and vulnerabilities about sharing the history of the failed marriage.

It is crucial to remember and to help the couple understand that both partners bring their own unique psychological and spiritual baggage. Each has her or his own complex history, assumptions, and expectations. Both bring fear and uncertainty, hope and commitment. They just come from different starting points.

- Refer to the section "Encouraging the Silent Partner, Working With the Talkative Partner" in chapter 4 for more guidance.

Cohabiting Couples

Couples who are living together and now seek a second marriage in the Church have some specific needs that should be addressed. *Getting Married, Living Together: A Guide for Engaged Couples* is a small resource booklet that will help you in working with these couples. Also, refer to the treatment of cohabitation in chapter 4 of this combined guide.

Death Versus Divorce

While two people may be entering a second marriage, if one does so following death and the other divorce, they will obviously be dealing with different concerns, fears, and doubts. It is important to keep these situations distinct. Those who are entering a second marriage after the first spouse has died will have particular grief issues. Sometimes there is lingering guilt about moving ahead in a new relationship. Sometimes there is fear of losing another spouse, especially if the first spouse died young or after a long and agonizing illness. Doubts about one's ability to handle the pain may remain. These will obviously need to be addressed, and you may want to explore additional resources from your parish's bereavement ministry.

Dealing with Resistance

From time to time you will encounter a couple or an individual who resists the process and makes it clear that he/she/they do not want to participate in a couple-to-couple program, or even in a private meeting with a pastoral minister.

In some cases there is underlying anger or resentment—unfinished anger from a previous marriage, unfinished anger at the annulment process (a person having to relive the pain of divorce, for example), or resentment at having to "jump through so many hoops" to have a civil marriage validated. Whatever the case, pay particular attention to any resistance that you encounter as it can make your task more difficult and the entire experience unpleasant for you and the couple you are assisting. Here are some behaviors that indicate that there might be resistance:

- Extended silences, especially after you have made attempts to involve the party

- Frequently passing when it is his or her turn to share

- Consistently answering questions in short, terse sentences

- Letting the fiancé answer for him or her

- Clear verbal challenges to having to participate in the program

- Disinterested body posture such as rolling of the eyes, looking away, sighing, and foot jiggling

- Talking to someone else during presentations, or simply not doing the requested exercises

In most cases resistance can be overcome by directly addressing the behaviors noticed as soon as possible. It is best not to let such behaviors go too long, as they can become entrenched and begin affecting all of your interactions with the engaged couple.

Reasons for resistance vary with each couple, as do appropriate pastoral responses from you as pastoral minister.

- Refer to the section "Dealing With Resistance" in chapter 4 of this *Combined Leader's Guide* for helpful hints.

CONFIDENTIALITY

When one or both engaged partners have lived through the pain of divorce or the death of a spouse, confidentiality often becomes a more significant issue than for those preparing for a first marriage. It is crucial to talk openly early in your working relationship with couples such as this about the ground rules. Particularly in the case of divorce, many people continue to feel a profound sense of failure for years. It is crucial that from the outset these couples hear you say, and come to trust, that their privacy is of fundamental concern to you.

- Refer to the section "Confidentiality" in chapter 4 for more guidance.

The Use of Professional Counseling in Preparing Couples for Remarriage in the Catholic Church

In many dioceses when a person is granted an annulment, there is an accompanying directive that the person receive some form of pastoral counseling before he or she can marry again or have an existing civil marriage validated in the Church. In many cases, a qualified pastoral counselor in a parish using the materials in *Catholic Remarriage* can meet this requirement. At other times, the couple or representatives of the Church will prefer the services of a professional family therapist. Having a referral list of qualified therapists readily available is important so that the couple can move forward with marriage preparation in a timely manner.

Many couples will agree to go to professional counseling to satisfy this directive, but keep in mind that counseling is often expensive and it might not be covered by insurance. Many pastoral ministers leave it up to the couple and marriage counselors as to the length of the counseling. One approach that seems to work well is to have the marriage counselor assess the strength and resiliency of the couple and address any glaring problems that may emerge. If the therapist finds that the couple has a high degree of marriage resiliency, then the counseling will be brief. If there are problems found in the assessment, then the counseling continues until these problems are addressed.

The Couple-to-Couple Approach

Sometimes a pastoral minister will refer a remarrying couple to a lead couple for part of the preparation. A good rule of thumb in this regard is to ask couples in your parish who have experienced the process of divorce, annulment, and remarriage to help with marriage preparation for these couples. The only caution with this is that you need to ensure that the couples you ask have a sound marriage, are committed to their faith, and are clear of any unfinished business due to divorce. Having a lead couple who knows the experience can be very helpful, especially if the couple to be married has any resistance or unresolved anger from the past.

FINALLY

In whatever situations and manner you use the material presented in *Catholic Remarriage: A Workbook for Couples*, keep in mind that the spiritual and emotional wounds that divorce or the death of a spouse brings will leave many people quite reluctant to talk. Even years after a marriage fails and a couple divorces, emotions can run high and egos remain fragile. Even years after the death of a spouse, grieving continues. As is the case with many beginning a first marriage, it is hard to underestimate the vulnerability of couples giving marriage a second try. This is true whether only one or both of the partners have been married before. Yet this vulnerability is remarkably mixed with hope, courage, and profound gratitude for the new life that has come with falling in love again.

Keep in mind that as someone helping couples prepare for a second marriage or convalidation, your role is really one of a trailblazer. The Church is just beginning to understand and publicly acknowledge the unique challenges that many married couples face. You are part of the growing wisdom on this matter. Your own experience is crucial in helping the Church address more adequately this developing and greatly needed area of pastoral ministry.

Prayers for the Engaged and Newly Married Couple

(Also available as prayer card downloads at avemariapress.com.)

A Prayer for a Passionate, Creative Love

Lord, send out your Spirit
and renew the face of the earth.
Father, Jesus gave his life
because he loved deeply and completely.
May our love for one another
be all encompassing and all consuming.
Make our love be pleasurable.
Make it be as creative as it is stable,
as passionate as it is respectful,
as gentle as it is strong,
so that all who know us will see in our
love the hand of you, our creator.
If and when we are blessed with children,
may they thrive in the passionate and energizing love
that has its beginning in the love you have for the world
and all its peoples.
We ask this through Jesus, our Lord and brother.
Amen.

A Prayer for Understanding

Lord, help us to always seek first

to understand each other, to lead with compassion,

and to walk a while in the other's experience.

Help us walk the road of marriage together,

trusting that when we doubt you will give us faith,

that when we criticize you will give us the courage to seek and offer forgiveness.

Make our love for one another burn in our hearts

in tough times as well as in the easy times.

May your Spirit renew our love again and again

so that we may give witness to your saving presence in our lives.

Amen.

A Prayer for Perseverance

Lord Jesus, in the garden of Gethsemane

you did not want to face the pain you knew would happen to you.

Yet you persevered and did not run from what lay ahead of you.

Guide us gently to face our fears.

Like your disciples in the storm-tossed boat,

we sometimes feel swamped by life's indifferent pressures.

May your presence always comfort us and lead us beyond fear to hope.

Help us to develop confidence in our own skills;

let us face our future with confidence in your sustaining presence.

Amen.

A Prayer to Tobias and Sarah

Tobias and Sarah, pray for us as we begin a life together.

You risked your reputation and your lives

for the sake of your love for each other.

Keep us faithful to our own journey of love.

Guide us to do what is right, not what others say is right.

May we be helpmates and partners to each other

and may God's Spirit keep us single-minded in our fidelity.

May your spirit teach us about energy and zeal for God's love;

as we walk our journey together may God's love always energize us.

Amen.

To Saints Anna and Joachim: On Children

We pray that our children will reach their full potential in the eyes of God,

as did your daughter Mary,

mother of Jesus our Lord.

May God's Holy Spirit lead us in the way of wonder and love

so that when we become parents

we will provide a home full of care, comfort, and structure.

Teach us to be a family that is holy,

one that sees in every person the dwelling place for God's Spirit.

As you taught your daughter Mary,

teach us to value our children for who they are,

not so much for what they can do.

May God keep us always loving and present

to the many joys, struggles, and hopes that our children possess.

Amen.

For Forgiveness: A Prayer to St. Peter

Peter, whom Jesus called Rock,

you know the pain and agony of having denied your friend and master.

Yet you were forgiven and called to mighty deeds.

Peter, you were married when Jesus called you to leave your nets and follow him.

Was your wife your silent partner?

Did she anchor you to reality when you dreamed wild schemes

and plans for the newborn church?

Did you have to seek her forgiveness for the excesses of your enthusiasm?

Pray for us, Rock of the Church,

when we fail our commitments

and even betray our friendship with each other.

Help us see that beyond the hurt and pain lies the grace of renewal.

As Jesus forgave you,

may we forgive each other and not harbor lasting resentment.

May our attitude always be as a child

who quickly forgets the hurt

because of the consoling presence of a loving friend.

We ask this through Jesus, our Lord and brother.

Amen.

A Prayer Concerning Conflict

Jesus, were there ever times when you became angry with your friends?

When you rebuked Peter and called him "Satan,"

were you angry because he tried to control what you were saying?

Show us that conflict can be holy ground,

that it need not be destructive.

Keep us honest and respectful of each other when we fight.

Lead us to take responsibility for our words and actions.

Remind us that we can always do better,

especially if we hit below the belt by name-calling and harsh criticism.

Above all else, send us your Spirit

to lead us in the way of respect and honesty,

so that our love may continue to deepen through the years.

Amen.

A Prayer to Abraham and Sarah

Abraham and Sarah, you risked all to journey to a new land you did not know.

And when you were old and beyond your childbearing years,

God granted your wish for a son.

You dared to dream, to laugh, and to hope in the promise of God.

Pray for us as we begin our journey of love.

Give us some of your vision.

May our dreams be rooted in the passion, perseverance, and humor

that the two of you possessed.

May God always lead us into our future.

Amen.

To Sarah, on Laughter

When the angel announced to Abraham
that you would bear a son,
you laughed because you were old and beyond your years.
Yet God laughed with you and gave you Isaac.
We pray that our marriage be for us a place of safety and a place of mirth.
May God keep our commitment to one another strong
and our love ever growing.
May we be able to laugh at ourselves
and not take ourselves too seriously.
With the help of the Spirit
may we transcend our limitations and sinfulness.
As we grow older, we pray that we, too,
can laugh and play in God's presence.
Amen.

The Covenant of Our Marriage

Father, you are creator of all things,
and you renew our commitments even when we fail
to keep our end of the covenant we make with you.
Keep us faithful to the covenant we enter together.
Help us realize that your sustaining presence
will guide us through the tough times that we will face.
When we are tempted to turn away from each other,
help us face our fears.
And when we want to blame the other for not meeting our needs,
teach us to take responsibility for ourselves.
Help us celebrate and proclaim
the lasting quality of our commitment to each other,
so that in seeing our love
others may see your presence.
Amen.

The Prayer of All Christians

Our Father,

who art in heaven,

hallowed be thy name;

thy kingdom come;

thy will be done

on earth as it is in heaven.

Give us this day our daily bread;

and forgive us our trespasses

as we forgive those who trespass against us;

and lead us not into temptation,

but deliver us from evil.

Amen.

1. "Introduction to the Rite of Marriage," in *The Rites* (New York: Pueblo Publishing, 1990), #7.

2. Ibid., #5.

3. *Familiaris Consortio* (Washington, DC: Office of Publishing Services, United States Catholic Conference, 1981), #66.

4. *Marriage Preparation in the Catholic Church*, Center for Marriage and Family, Creighton University, November 1995, p. 27.

5. *Familiaris Consortio*, #73.

6. *Faithful to Each Other Forever* (Washington, DC: Committee for Pastoral Research and Practices, National Conference of Catholic Bishops, 1989), p. 60.

7. Ibid., p. 60.

8. Ibid., p. 61.

9. Joseph M. Champlin, *The Marginal Catholic* (Notre Dame, IN: Ave Maria Press, 1989), pp. 138–39.

10. *Faithful to Each Other Forever*, p. 62. See also: Code of Canon Law, c. 1077.

11. *Faithful to Each Other Forever*, p. 151.

12. Ibid., p. 40.

13. Ibid., p. 60.

14. Ibid., p. 63.

15. *Marriage Preparation in the Catholic Church*, p. 46.

16. Michael F. Pennock, *This Is Our Faith* (Notre Dame, IN: Ave Maria Press, 1998).

17. Patricia Morrison Driedger, *The Church: Our Story* (Notre Dame, IN: Ave Maria Press, 1999, 2006).

18. "Introduction to the Rite of Marriage," #1 and 2.

19. *Catechism of the Catholic Church*, Liberia Editrice Vaticana, #1617.

20. *Faithful to Each Other Forever*, p. 78.

21. Ibid., p. 78.

22. Ibid., p. 78.

23. Ibid., p. 71.

24. Ibid., p. 73.

25. *Familiaris Consortio*, #81.

26. See Peter Kline and Bernard Saunders, *Ten Steps to a Learning Organization* (Arlington, VA: Great Ocean Publishers, 1993), p. 61.

27. See John Gottman, *Why Marriages Fail or Succeed* (New York: Fireside, 1994).

Anthony Garascia, clinical director of the Samaritan Counseling Center in South Bend, Indiana, has over twenty years experience in marriage and family counseling. He holds a master's degree in counseling from Indiana University and a master of arts degree in Liturgical Studies from the Catholic University of America. Garascia is a regular workshop presenter and author of *Getting Married, Living Together*; *Rekindle the Passion While Raising Your Kids*; and *Catholic Remarriage* (Ave Maria Press). He and his wife, Beth, have three grown children.

Susan Vogt is author of books and articles on marriage, parenting, and spirituality. She worked for over thirty years as a diocesan family life director and was a lay advisor to the USCCB Committee on Marriage and Family. She is the mother of four young adult children and resides in Covington, Kentucky, with her husband, Jim.

Marriage Resources

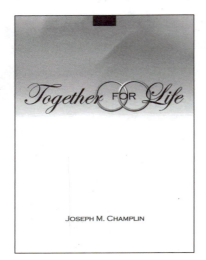

Together for Life

Rev. Joseph M. Champlin

As the most popular and most complete resource of its kind, *Together for Life* enables couples to plan and participate actively in their wedding liturgy, while challenging them to reflect together on the sacred commitment of marriage. The *Special Edition* for marriage outside Mass is identical to the *Regular Edition* with the exception that it omits all references to the Nuptial Mass.

REGULAR EDITION: ISBN: 9780877936169 / 96 pages, photos / $3.50
SPECIAL EDITION: ISBN: 9780877936176 / 96 pages, photos / $3.50

FEATURES:

- Couples are encouraged to actively participate in planning and personalizing their wedding liturgy
- All authorized readings, prayers, prefaces, and blessings included
- 4-page tear-out selection sheet to submit to priest or marriage coordinator
- Inspiring commentaries for each reading for couples to reflect on the significance of their commitment
- "How to Plan Your Wedding" section dedicated to helping couples understand the basic structure of the wedding liturgy

View sample pages online at **www.avemariapress.com**

Together for Life E-Newsletter

ave maria press is happy to offer a **FREE** quarterly e-newsletter providing encouragement and support for newly married couples.

Each e-newsletter issue contains:

- Practical insight and wisdom from well-known Catholic marriage professionals
- Real-life stories from newly married couples
- Advice on enriching the spiritual dimensions of newly married life together
- Special reflections by Father Joseph Champlin

FREE! Subscribe online at **www.avemariapress.com**
Look for the *Together for Life* E-Newsletter Link

ave maria press
Notre Dame, IN 46656 • Ph: 800-282-1865
www.avemariapress.com
A Ministry of the Indiana Province of Holy Cross
Also available from your bookstore

Keycode: F0A0807000